A L   J A N D L

Al Jandl is known as a pastor's pastor and a visionary leader for the 21st century. From humble beginnings as a store manager for a major grocery chain, Al Jandl has become a nationally known pastor, conference speaker, and leader.

In 1975, Reverend Jandl founded Living Stones Church in Alvin, Texas. Today, Living Stones is one of America's outstanding churches known for its spirit of excellence and life-changing message of stability and personal growth. Under his leadership, the Living Stones family of ministries has acquired 280 acres in the city of Alvin and has developed a significant outreach to the greater Alvin area with a roster of community service projects and corporate clients. Besides Living Stones Church, these ministries also include Living Stones Christian School (a fully accredited K-12 school), Precious Stones Day Care, and the state-of-the-art Victory Camp—-an outstanding resource for reaching people with the Gospel, especially young people, and consisting of impeccable lodging, meeting, cafeteria and entertainment facilities.

Al's life is an example of a man who simply called out to God for help, and then watched as God made that moment a turning point in his life. Reverend Jandl has authored numerous books.

His wife of over 27 years, Judy, is principal of Living Stones Christian School. They have two daughters, Jessica and Stephanie, who also serve on the faculty there.

VAN CROUCH

Van Crouch is widely regarded as one of the best and most versatile speakers in America. As the founder and president of the consulting firm, Van Crouch Communications, Van challenges individuals to achieve excellence in their lives.

In Van's experiences in the corporate arena and as a speaker to many of the nation's professional and collegiate sports teams, he exudes an enthusiasm for life, a spontaneous sense of humor, and a genuine interest in people.

After ranking as a consistent sales leader with the American Express Company, Van went on to receive many awards for outstanding performance in the insurance industry and has been a qualifying member of the Million Dollar Round Table.

Van is in demand for his thought-provoking seminars and keynote engagements with Fortune 500 companies, governmental organizations, professional sports teams, church groups, and management and sales conventions worldwide. Van has also authored the best-selling books *Stay in the Game*, *Winning 101*, and *Dare to Succeed*.

Van Crouch has the ability to motivate people to raise their level of expectation. He will inspire you so that your attitude will become more positive, your problems smaller, your self-esteem and confidence greater, and your self-doubts will disintegrate. He is sure to both inspire and challenge you with his writings.

Van resides in Wheaton, Illinois with his wife, Doni, who is also active in the ministry. They have four grown children.

Here's what other key leaders and organizations have said over the last 25 years about Al Jandl and Van Crouch.

"Al Jandl has an incredible depth of rich biblical insight that has positively impacted my personal life and that of our academic community."

—**Dr. Oral Roberts, Chancellor**
Oral Roberts University

"Van Crouch relates Christian principles to contemporary problems with clarity and conviction. Splendid speaker!" —**Paul Harvey**
American Broadcasting Company (ABC)

"Here's hoping, Van, the day will come when we are able to do some work together. You do a marvelous job. God bless you and your activities."

—**Zig Ziglar**
Zig Ziglar Corporation

"Van, you have not only challenged and inspired us, but you have enabled us to more insightfully seek God's plan in both our personal and professional lives. We appreciate the new perspective that you've given us through your ministry to us, and certainly we wholeheartedly appreciate you. Your selfless attitude, which displays an eagerness to serve the Lord in whatever capacity He calls you, will remain for us an example that we should all do well to follow." —**Dr. James Dobson, Ph.D., Founder**
Focus on the Family

"We hope you were blessed as much as we were by your recent appearance on Life Today. Thank you for your willingness to share from the heart. We have a potential viewing audience of more than 100 million households, so imagine the impact your message can have!"

—**James Robison, President & CEO**
Life Today

"What a special delight to meet you! Thanks for your enthusiastic, exhilarating, and informative message to the CBA Future of the Industry conference! ... Thanks again, Van, for your personal interest in CBA and the unique ministry God has called us to in this industry.... I keep finding myself engrossed with the practical directness with which you present the concepts."

—William R. Anderson, President
Christian Booksellers Association—CBA
Colorado Springs, Colorado

"Your gracious and generous contribution to our ministry is still an awesome wonder in all of our minds and hearts. God did a great work in your meeting. You're one of our modern-day heroes. We love you, admire you, respect you, and esteem you highly for the Gospel's sake."

—Dr. Edwin Louis Cole
Christian Men's Network

"It is so encouraging to know that God has choice servants representing Jesus Christ in the marketplace. Your input was exciting and challenging. Thanks again for co-laboring with us in such a strategic ministry reaching out to the marketplace."

—Rev. Richard A. Duncan, Pastor of Evangelism
The Moody Church
Chicago, Illinois

"Van Crouch is one of America's great speakers and authors. His amazing humor combined with practical and biblical insight will have you not only encouraged, but empowered! *The Storehouse Principle* is a must read for all those desiring to change their financial future TODAY!"

—Gregory M. Dickow, Founder and Senior Pastor
Life Changers International Church
Chicago, Illinois

"I'm just thankful that Van Crouch isn't an NFL linebacker, because he is the hardest-hitting speaker I've ever heard." **—Walter Payton**
Chicago Bears, NFL
Football Hall of Fame

"The coaches, players and staff of the Chicago Bears truly appreciate your interest, leadership and time spent in furthering and interpreting the 'Good News.' It is our wish that you will continue to help and inspire our players in the coming year. Thank you again for a job well done."

—Mike Ditka, Former Head Football Coach
Chicago Bears, NFL
Super Bowl XX Champions

"You are truly a professional. Your eloquent message mixed practical application, knowledge, skill and information with timely quotes and humor. You're a dedicated professional, a salesman, a humorist, and a minister. Our people loved your presentation."

—Ken Thul, Vice-President of Sales
Catholic Aid Association

"Thank you for making our prayer luncheon an overwhelming success. This luncheon was the most successful of its kind and is due in large measure to your ability to captivate, motivate, and inform your listeners. Your unique approach of presenting scriptural principles through humor delighted our audience."   **—Donald R. Infante, Major General, U.S. Army**
Department of the Army
El Paso, Texas

"Thank you for your contribution to our National Renewal Conference...we feel the meeting was very successful. God's presence was truly felt as He blessed us in many ways. Van, your part was excellent. It was humorous but yet very much to the point of Christian commitment."

—Leonard Hinton, Reid Hardin, Jim Rogers, Home Mission Board
Southern Baptist Convention (SBC)
Atlanta, Georgia

"We were most fortunate to have acquired the services of a person such as yourself. You have played an expanded role towards our winning tradition. Thank you for your efforts."   **—Tom Landry, Former Head Coach**
Dallas Cowboys

"Pat Robertson has asked me to thank you personally for your recent appearance on The 700 Club. Pat and all of us at CBN believe that God is using the insights you shared to comfort and encourage those in our viewing audience." — **Jackie Mitchum, 700 Club Guest Coordinator**
The 700 Club
Virginia Beach, Virginia

"Your sincerity and knowledge of sales, coupled with your professional platform ability, make you a very unique speaker. I knew you were going to be good, but am glad to say you far surpassed what we were expecting. Thanks again for making all of our lives better and I hope you will have the privilege of doing the same for many, many more people."

—Charles E. "Tremendous" Jones, President
Life Management Services, Inc.
Harrisburg, Pennsylvania

"Thank you so much for being available to minister at the Marketplace Ministry meeting and our Sunday services. Words cannot express how grateful I am.... The people who attended are still talking about what a wonderful time they had and how much they have learned as a result of your ministry time with us."

—Art Sepulveda, Pastor
Word of Life Christian Center
Honolulu, Hawaii

"Your talk to the Texaco Superstars group last week was one of the highlights of the trip. Your great sense of humor combined with your motivational comments had the audience alternatively 'rolling in the aisles' and seriously contemplating your inspiring message. It is not often that a speaker can hit exactly the right keys in an address, but you certainly did on this occasion." — **J.W. "Bill" Beard**
Texaco
Houston, Texas

"Our people were full of positive comments and upbeat reaction to the highly entertaining way you got your message across to us. Your five points will help us remember how to apply and make that difference on the job and in our own lives." **— John J. Puljung, District Manager/External Affairs AT&T**

"Van delivered a motivational message that combined humor and inspiration. The response from the group was very positive. Our business is both demanding and competitive. Van provided the very positive closing touch that sent everyone home feeling great." **—Rhonda M. Woodard Allstate Northbrook, Illinois**

"I wanted to take this opportunity on behalf of American Airlines, Flight Service, to express our sincere appreciation for the valuable presentation you made to our organization. Van, I would be remiss if I did not mention that few... if any speakers have ever received a 'standing ovation,' you did... and that meant true success. What a moment!! We sincerely thank you for becoming a part of our team and exceeding the challenge to achieve excellence." **— Trina Paxton, Manager Flight Service American Airlines**

"Van is an expert at encouraging others to creatively address the future with a sense of personal responsibility while inspiring them to believe in worthwhile results. Van's gift for motivating people to raise their level of expectation is a challenge and an inspiration." **—The Salvation Army**

"Without exception, our supervisors and department heads were motivated by your enthusiastic talk. You did a truly outstanding job."

—L. Ronald Johnson, CTC Delta Air Lines, Inc. Schaumburg, Illinois

"We've never been graced by a more dynamic speaker. From the opening line, everyone was gripped by the humor and the message of hope presented. We'll remember that evening as a time where we heard a word from the Lord, and were motivated to follow it."

—**Rev. Richard Valkanet, Executive Director**
Chicago Teen Challenge
Chicago, Illinois

"You did a wonderful job of teaching, challenging, and uplifting. Special thanks for your warmth, humor, and enthusiasm. All contributed to your message and added impact. You're very special!"

—**Randy St. Clair, Vice President/National Program Activities**
Fellowship of Christian Athletes (FCA)
Kansas City, Missouri

"I thank you again for coming to speak to the Vols at our chapel. Your message was very inspirational and informative and our team and staff enjoyed it very much. The Tennessee Vols appreciate you very much. We continue to grow in God's Word with men like you leading the way."

—**Phillip Fulmer, Head Football Coach**
University of Tennessee
Knoxville, Tennessee

"As the founder and president of a private investment firm, I transact with many successful CEO's and Captains of Industry. However, I have never met a more visionary man than Pastor Al Jandl. His teachings and pragmatic sense of monetary values and growth will guide you through a lifetime of comfort and asset preservation."

—**J. David Salinas**
J. David Financial Group

AL JANDL
and
VAN CROUCH

with RICK KILLIAN

THE
STOREHOUSE
PRINCIPLE

A Revolutionary God Idea for Creating
Extraordinary Financial Stability

CROSSSTAFF
PUBLISHERS, LLC

BOULDER · ST. PAUL · TULSA

Published in Broken Arrow, Oklahoma, by CrossStaff Publishers, LLC

Manuscript prepared by Rick Killian, Killian Creative, Boulder, Colorado.
www.killiancreative.com

Cover & ineterior: Lookout Design Group, Inc., Minneapolis, Minnesota
www.lookoutdesign.com

Published in association with Yates & Yates, L.L.P.,
Attorneys and Counselors, Orange, California.

ISBN 0-9743876-0-6

Printed in the United States of America
12 11 10 09 08 07 06 05 04   10 9 8 7 6 5 4 3 2 1

To a wonderful friend, mentor and pastor

John Osteen
August 21, 1921 – January 23, 1999

The late John Osteen served the Lord Jesus Christ as a pastor, evangelist, author, and teacher for sixty years. His ministry became a worldwide outreach for Jesus Christ. He traveled extensively throughout the world, taking the message of God's love, healing and power to people of all nations.

John Osteen founded Lakewood Church in Houston, Texas, widely known as "The Oasis of Love in a Troubled World," where his family continues to minister to thousands weekly. He hosted the weekly "John Osteen" television program for 16 years, reaching millions in the U.S. and in many other countries with the Gospel.

...He "served God's purpose in
his own generation." —Acts 13:36 NIV

CONTENTS

PART THREE: *(A Closing Message from Al and Van)*
Putting It All Together: Living Out the Storehouse Blessing

INTRODUCTION

by Van Crouch

How's your financial life going? Is it moving along as well as you think it should? Or do you feel like you are in a gang fight and your gang didn't show up? It's tough wandering through life like a piano player in a marching band.

Are you confident about your future? Or do you have doubts? Are you leaving a mark on the world around you? When your life ends, what legacy will you leave behind? What a tragedy it would be to live an entire life without ever realizing the fulfillment and rewards that come from reaching our full potential.

Have you lowered your aspirations and settled for mediocrity? Have you decided to just maintain the status quo in your life instead of charging ahead of the pack? Are you groping for ways to get ahead in today's volatile and uncertain economy?

These were some of the thoughts going through my mind as the United Airlines Airbus A319 I was on winged its way toward Houston's George Bush Intercontinental Airport. The Alvin, Texas Chamber of Commerce had invited me to speak at a banquet honoring their police department. It was to become a night that would change my life forever.

The name, "Al Jandl", kept coming up as I crisscrossed the country from meeting to meeting. His name was synonymous with excellence in ministry. Pastor Jandl was to host the police banquet and I was very excited to meet him. Al is known as a visionary leader with a great gift for conducting business by the book, i.e. the Bible.

Although I had had some interesting assignments in my career, my financial bottom line did not reflect success in the way that it should have. I had begun my career as a college football coach and later served as a player personnel scout for the Dallas Cowboys. God was very gracious to open the door for me to be a pre-game inspirational speaker for most of the nation's major league baseball teams as well as NFL football teams.

My corporate career began with the American Express Company in Chicago. My sales territory was so tough that when Al Capone lived there he worked as an Avon lady! The police department had an unlisted telephone number! But I experienced success, and as a national sales leader for American Express, I was given the opportunity to join its management team. Later, as a life insurance agent for New York Life and Northwestern Mutual, I was a Qualifying Member of the Million Dollar Round Table. After a few years in business, a window of opportunity opened for me as a public speaker for major businesses and organizations, and I had a Fortune 500 list of clients such as American Airlines, American Express, Allstate, AT&T, the Chicago Bears, Farm Bureau, Gold Medal, IBM, National Association of Life Underwriters, State Farm, and Texaco. From the locker room to the corporate board room, I was there.

Unfortunately, none of these career highlights produced any sustained financial stability. As a Christian, I had heard and begun to practice the Bible principle of tithing and giving offerings—of seedtime and harvest. But something was missing! Often, my outgo exceeded my income and caused my upkeep to become my downfall! In my family tree there was absolutely no financial legacy to imitate. My grandparents said things were so tough for them that when the Great Depression of 1929 hit, they began to sing, "Let the Good Times Roll!"

Many business and financial books focus on success and present examples you can't relate to. You may be impressed, even awed, by someone's brilliant financial strategy, but end up frustrated if you're not able to apply it in your own life. It's not necessarily inspiring to read about other people's success when your own life seems to rival Job's. The end result of too many of the positive books becomes negative because you can wind up feeling deficient. I really needed help, a key, some direction. The answer was not another "How to Do It" book but a living example. For me, that answer came in the person of Al Jandl.

You are about to meet two men who encountered the God of Jeremiah 32:27, "Behold, I am the Lord, the God of all flesh; is there anything too hard for me?"

Listen to Al Jandl as he shares how the power of Jesus Christ changed his life and helped him to dig deep into God's plan for financial stability.

It's not too late! Anyone can begin to practice the "Storehouse Principle" at anytime, anywhere. Stand back and watch hope arise as this revolutionary God idea begins to create extraordinary financial peace and stability in your heart and life.

God's best is yours!

PART ONE

AL´S STORY:

UNDERSTANDING THE

STOREHOUSE PRINCIPLE

1

A REVOLUTIONARY GOD IDEA

**The LORD will command the blessing on you in your
storehouses and in all to which you set your hand,
and He will bless you in the land which the LORD
your God is giving you.**

DEUTERONOMY 28:8 NKJV

If you'd told me when I was growing up that there would come a
day in my life when I would stop worrying about having enough
money, I would have thought you were crazy. If you'd told me that I'd
have enough to fulfill my dreams, I am sure I would have laughed in
your face. That's just the way I grew up. If I ever had two nickels to
rub together as a child, I don't remember it. My mother would do
anything she could to pinch a penny. Everything that we ever did—
or didn't do—as far as I remember—was to stretch what little money
we had.

For one thing, I remember that Saturday night was always bath
night. There were five kids in my family and all of us would take a
bath in only two tubs of water—a couple in the first and then the rest
of us in the other. Then the next morning I would go to church and

the minister would tell us how blessed the poor were—but I felt anything but blessed!

We almost always wore second or third-hand clothes and shoes. When there weren't hand-me-down shoes available, Mom would go to a discount store and buy shoes for us. I think she used to get two pairs for $3.99. Even though they were new, they never seemed to last very long. I remember one pair I had where the sole came loose—it would catch on the ground and then flap back up against the bottom of my foot making sort of a quacking noise. The other kids at school started saying things like "There goes that kid with the duck shoes again." I was so embarrassed I wanted to die. I tried tying them up with string and putting rubber bands around them to keep them shut, but the string and rubber bands would only wear away and eventually break. There wasn't anything else I could do because we had no money to get another pair. So I learned to live with the "quack" as I walked and the mocking laughter that always followed.

We always needed money. Mom was always after us to turn out the lights, shut off the water, or do something else to keep our bills down. I grew up poor, and figured I would be poor the rest of my life. I had never known anything else, so I never expected anything better.

Yet One Revelation Can Change Everything

Someone once told me that you are only one revelation away from a miracle. It was just such a revelation that changed all of that forever. Though the revelation came quickly, I was so backward in my thinking at the time that the miracle took several years to develop. It is my hope, however, that once you understand this revolutionary principle from God's Word, it will work faster for you than it has for me, just as it has for many I have shared it with over the years.

The revelation of the Storehouse Principle in my life starts in 1974, when I began serving as an interim pastor for a small church near Alvin, Texas. Before that time, I had spent several years successfully climbing the career ladder in a major grocery store chain where I had worked since I was a teenager. I liked my work there and thought I was pretty good at it. It was really about the only thing I was good at—the rest of my life during that time was a miserable mess. I had gotten into so much trouble that except for the grace of God I would have been dead a couple of times over before I reached my 31st birthday.

But on May 18th of 1972, at the age of 32, I finally gave my life completely over to God. Things started to change quickly after that. First of all, even though I had planned to be a big shot for the grocery chain, I completely lost my desire to continue working for them. I felt that God was calling me into the ministry. So a few weeks later I resigned, found a new job somewhere else, and started learning everything about God that I could.

Obeying God Brings Dramatic Changes

That eventually led me to my sister's home in Escondido, California in early June of 1974 with no home, no job, and no prospects. I had sold my house in the Houston area and was planning to use the profit from that to go on a missionary trip to India. It seemed so odd, but I felt strongly that it was what God wanted me to do. I had no idea what else I would be doing except to go on that trip in October. I had nothing in the world except my 1970 Plymouth Duster, a box of books in its trunk, a little money in the bank left over from my days working in the grocery business, and a suitcase full of clothes.

I didn't have anything to do while I was at my sister's house, which always makes me restless. My sister and her husband were working, so I didn't even have anyone to talk with while they were away. I decided that I might as well spend a couple of hours reading. I went to the trunk of my car, rummaged through my box of books, and pulled out a copy of *The Cross and the Switchblade* by David Wilkerson. I remember going back into the house and sitting down on the couch with the sunshine streaming through the window thinking I would read until my sister or her husband got home, but I had another thing coming.

As my eyes passed over the words on the first few pages of the book, I found them filling with tears. I couldn't stop crying. Something powerful had gripped my heart and wouldn't let go. Finally, I couldn't see the pages to read, so I set the book down. For the rest of the day I kept crying off and on. I had no idea what was wrong with me.

The next day everything seemed better, until I sat down in the early afternoon to try to read that book again. My eyes passed over the same few words and again the tears came. I didn't know what to do, but I also knew it was something from God. So I went back into the room where I was staying and prayed, "Why am I crying like this? What is this all about?" Eventually I felt a burden in my heart that God wanted me to return to Alvin, Texas and become a pastor. I had no idea what that meant, but knew it was God. So I put down the book, gathered up my things, called my sister to say good-bye, and drove through the night toward Alvin which was not far from where I had lived before in the Houston area.

God Had Bigger Plans for Me

I arrived there on a Saturday and found out that that night there was a Christian businessmen's meeting at an old theatre building in Alvin, so I decided to check it out. At that meeting, a pastor got up and asked the crowd if they knew of any ministers who could take over his church, because he had resigned and was planning on leaving it after the morning service the next day. No one said anything—especially me—but as he said that, I felt the same burden in my heart I had felt while I was praying in California. I remember walking the streets of Alvin after that meeting praying, "God don't leave those people without a pastor. You can't leave them without a pastor, God. You have to get somebody to pastor that church."

The next morning I went to that church. It was the craziest place I had ever seen. It had brown contact paper covering the windows.

The only light in it came from four bare bulbs hanging from the ceiling, and there were dingy vinyl tiles on the floor. If ever a place could look depressed, it did. The pastor got up that day and preached a sermon that criticized the congregation for their lack of zeal for God and encouragement for their pastor. They just sat there, taking it all in, hardly moving a muscle. I guess I could see at that point why he was resigning.

I didn't talk with anyone that day at the church. I left right after the service ended—it was really more like I ran out—and tried not to give it another thought. However, within a few days I was making $20 a week as the interim pastor for that church. I wasn't a preacher, I hadn't been to seminary, and I wasn't ordained, but since I was available, God used me to meet their need.

God Provided for My Needs

Since I had no home, I slept on the couch in the front room of a home that belonged to a sweet, older woman in the church. She took me in as if she were my grandmother. It was one of those little shotgun houses where the whole house wasn't much wider than that couch. Despite the scant circumstances, within just a few months, God hit that church with a revival. Out of the people who were saved in that revival, Living Stones Church was born, where I still serve as the Senior Pastor today. Believe it or not, our first meetings took place in that little old shotgun house. I still could not tell you today how we all fit into it!

Despite the fact that I was now a pastor and the church had accepted me as their leader, I felt like I didn't know anything about God nor what it meant to be a pastor. I was also still incredibly hungry for God. Since I only had a small congregation, and not much money to cover more than the most basic necessities, I didn't do much besides read my Bible and pray—which I probably did for eight to twelve hours per day. I wanted to learn everything that I could about God.[1]

Eventually, I found my own place to live and met a beautiful woman, Judy, whom I married on August 13, 1976. I remember that by then I was earning $75 a week, and the congregation was meeting in an old church that had been built around 1900. As a married man, I was concerned about the future more than ever before. My salary didn't go very far, and although Judy owned a dress shop with her mother, the shop hadn't made money for years. It had been very successful when it was the only one in Alvin, but a mall opened up nearby, and sales began to slump. Judy's father had died some years before and all Judy and her mother had for income was that dress shop. Her mother had borrowed money for the past five years to keep it afloat, and when Judy's mother eventually remarried, she turned the store completely over to Judy just before she and I were married.

---

[1] In the last chapter of this book we've included some of these scriptures for your own study.

Stability Brings Responsibility

At that time, I still had about $2,000 left over from my days working in the grocery chain, and I used half of that to pay for our honeymoon. When we returned, we started accumulating debt both personally and with the dress shop. Suddenly, all the memories of growing up poor came back to haunt me and I felt helpless. I knew if we didn't make some changes soon that we would be heading for bankruptcy—but I didn't have any idea what those changes should be. As each day went by, I felt more and more desperate. I was the poorest person in my church and I felt like I was getting poorer by the minute.

Because of this, I went down to the church building to fast and pray for three days about what we were supposed to do. I stayed there listening to teaching tapes, reading my Bible, and walking the aisles praying. After two and a half days, I got what I thought was my answer. I felt that God wanted me to give away the last $1,000 I had left in savings. He wanted me to give $500 to one woman from our church, and He led me to give away the rest a short time later.

Since I felt like I had heard an answer to my prayers, I didn't wait any longer but went home and told my wife what I felt we were to do. She agreed, and we gave away the money. I also went to the dress shop and took some of our best and most expensive merchandise and gave that away as well.

We suddenly had nothing left but our debt and our God. God

must have wanted us to know that everything that happened after that point was because of Him, because we had no one and nothing else to depend upon.

A Simple, Revolutionary God Idea

So we went back to work, and we worked hard. In addition to my responsibilities at the church, I was spending more and more time in the evenings at the dress shop, and also continued reading my Bible several hours a day. Then one day as I was reading in Deuteronomy chapter 28, I came across this scripture:

> The LORD will command the blessing
> on you in your storehouses and in all to which
> you set your hand, and He will bless you in the land
> which the LORD your God is giving you.
>
> DEUTERONOMY 28:8 NKJV

After I had read it, I went back to the start of chapter 28 and read it from the beginning again. I noticed that verse 8 had a word in it that none of the other verses on blessing had—the word *command*.

Well, I thought, *if God is going to* command *a blessing on my store-houses, then I had better have some.* That was it. It wasn't a big deal or a flash of lightning, but at that thought I felt a sudden surge of hope inside of me. I decided at that moment I would start a storehouse for the church, and one for my wife and me, personally. It was a simple decision to obey what I had read in the Word of God.

Little did I know that it would also be the seed of revelation that would change the course of our ministry, my opinion of myself, and the way I looked at money for the rest of my life. The Lord led Judy and me to lay the foundation for our storehouse by first giving things away and making a fresh start. He may lead others in a different way, but the key is to obey Him as He guides us and to put the principles of His Word into effect. The result in our lives has been abundant blessing, and God has been faithful to enable us to live debt free.

2

"LETTUCE" IN THE VEGETABLE BIN

**In my trouble (poverty) I have prepared
for the house of the LORD.**

1 CHRONICLES 22:14 *(insert added)*

When I told the members of my church board that I was going to start saving money for the church in a storehouse, they agreed, but then they asked me where I was going to find any extra money to save. Our church barely had enough to cover our normal expenses! When I started looking around for some area of the church where we had a little extra money from time to time, it took me a while to find something.

What I finally discovered was the church book table. We bought and sold books that helped people learn more about God at a small table in the entryway of the church, and of course, we bought the books at a discount, so we made a little bit of profit from each one we sold. I decided to start saving that money for the church rather than just putting it into the general expense account. It wasn't much, so I knew we wouldn't really miss it.

Doing this, it took me about two months to save a hundred dollars. I remember reaching that point, because when it totaled one hundred dollars, I took all of the loose bills and change and exchanged it for a one-hundred-dollar bill.

Our First Storehouse

When I was growing up, my mother told me, "Al, if you ever get extra money, put it under the vegetable bin in the refrigerator. If a thief ever comes into your house, he will never think to look there, and if there is a fire, the last place that will burn will be the inside of the refrigerator—so it is the safest place in the house!" So I took the hundred-dollar bill, put it inside a plastic bag, placed it with the other "lettuce" in the refrigerator, and didn't think much of it again.

It's not very scientific, but that was the beginning of our church's storehouse. I didn't know what it would be used for, I just knew from Deuteronomy 28 that I was supposed to save money for the church. I figured when the time came, God would let me know what to do with it. I was just obeying what God had shown me to do, so we were saving money. But, putting that money into our refrigerator was also changing me—it gave me a sense of accomplishment, so I started getting diligent about saving it.

King David's Storehouse

I later found out that I was echoing something the Bible tells us that David did.

Now, behold, in my trouble I have prepared for the house
of the LORD an hundred thousand talents of gold, and a
thousand thousand talents of silver;
and of brass and iron without weight; for it is
in abundance: timber also and stone have I prepared;
and thou mayest add thereto.

1 CHRONICLES 22:14

If you look in the margin of most *King James* Bibles or even in your *Strong's Concordance*, you will see that the word "trouble" also means "poverty." In other words, David started saving money and supplies to build a temple for God even when it wasn't convenient or easy to do. The *New American Standard Bible* says it this way: "with great pains I have prepared for the house of the LORD," or, in other words, he began storing this up and it took quite a bit of work and effort to do it! In essence, we were doing the same thing for our church. When we had little to speak of, we started putting something into our storehouse, little by little.

Our Storehouse Multiplied

Over the next eight to ten months, I saved nine more one-hundred-dollar bills. When it reached that much, Judy said to me, "Al, this isn't the best place for this money. Why don't you let me put it in the safe deposit box down at the bank?" I said, "Sure," so she took those ten one-hundred-dollar bills all wrapped up in a plastic bag with a rubber band around them down to the bank and put them in the church's safe deposit box.

Now, other than just keeping it, I still didn't know what the money was for, nor did I discuss how much we had saved with anyone in the church. I was afraid that if I told anyone that I had saved $1,000 of the church's money, someone would get upset with me! I was so used to having nothing that now having a savings seemed extravagant. But all of this time, God was still working on me. Having this diligence to save and having something in the bank for the church started to slowly change the way I looked at things. We were no longer "broke." We had something, even if it was only a little. We had a financial foundation and I no longer had to worry about paying the church bills each week the way I used to because we suddenly had some reserves. I still didn't want to touch the money if I could help it, but having that little bit in the bank made me sleep better at night.

From Savings to Investing

Then a few weeks later, Judy said to me again, "You know, Al, that money isn't doing any good just sitting there in the safe deposit box. Why don't you let me put it in a savings account so that it can begin to earn a little interest?" I agreed again, and she went down to the bank to open a savings account for the church.

You might not believe this, but when my beautiful, usually calm and loving wife came back from the bank she said, "Next time you're going to the bank yourself!" When I asked her what was wrong, she gave me "that" look.

"I was so embarrassed!" she told me. "I got the money in the plastic bag out of the safe deposit box and brought it around to the teller and handed it to her. She took it, pulled off the rubber band, and then made an awful face as she took the money out of the bag. 'This is the funniest money I have ever seen!' she told me. 'It feels so weird—and it smells!' I looked at the money and it was black with mildew on it. I was so embarrassed. From now on, you can go yourself with your money to put it in the bank!"

Of course, we both laugh when we look back on that now, but what a way to start! The church now had its first thousand dollars in a storehouse account. While that was going on, she and I were trying to build our own personal storehouse as well, though it wasn't growing as fast and the dress shop was still struggling.

The Principle Begins to Sink In

By this time, I was beginning to see that there really was something to having a storehouse. It wasn't some magic wand to wave over our finances and make everything better, but somehow it was much more than just saving money—it was obeying God's Word and then allowing Him to work His wisdom in our lives so that worrying about paying our bills wasn't an all-consuming thing anymore. Getting more money was no longer a major focus. Our focus was on getting more of God's wisdom. We began seeing that this principle was affecting every area of our lives. Before we bought anything new for ourselves, we began to ask, "Do we really need this, or would it be better to take the money we would spend and put it into the storehouse?" We became more frugal and found ways to get things without spending all of our money or going into debt. If we needed something, we would save for it until we had enough money for it, and then often found that we didn't need it after all, so we would just put the money in the bank!

This didn't happen all at once, but this attitude became more and more a part of us as we saw what was happening with the church's storehouse as well as our own. I remember telling Judy early on that we would never borrow money again, not even to buy a house, and her first thought was, *Well, then we will never own a house!*

A New Attitude Toward Extra Money

Yet, shortly after we started all of this, Judy's grandmother made the decision to start distributing some of her grandchildren's inheritance to them before she died. She had some investments, and let Judy know one day that she should start expecting to get a check from that every month or so. When we heard that, we thought, *Now that could sure help us with the dress shop*, but then realized that dumping that into the shop would be like dumping it into a hole in the ground—the dress shop needed to take care of itself. So I told her, "We didn't have that money to live off of before, so we can do without it now. Why don't we just start putting it away into the storehouse each month, after we pay our tithe, and not think about it again?" Judy agreed, so we started to save that money each month rather than just blowing it on something we didn't really need.

Becoming Even More Diligent

Meanwhile, the dress shop was slumping even further. It finally got to the point where the vendors wouldn't sell us the next season's line of clothing because the shop wasn't bringing in enough money. We were trying to sell last summer's swimsuits in the middle of winter. It was bad. The accountant even told us that we would be bankrupt within the next year, but we both said, "No, we won't!"

We kept praying over the shop and applying what God was teaching us to manage it. We searched the Bible for God's promises on success for our business and put our trust in Him for them to take place. We quoted those scriptures out loud to each other all of the time when we were together at the store to keep our faith on what God had promised in His Word. I remember one day all we sold was a scarf for $6.00 and it just about killed any hope I had had for the store. But I went home and got my attitude right, and went back to the shop again the next day believing God was going to show us how to make it work. We didn't give up.

So we became more and more diligent in managing the store. After my work at the church, I would go to the store and rearrange the merchandise every few days. Regular customers would see things in the store and say, "Oh, this is lovely! Did you just get it in?" when it had been in the store for a couple of months or so. Because the things had been rearranged, they were attracted to it like it was new and would buy it. We were again seeing the commanded blessing of Deuteronomy 28:8—in addition to blessing our storehouses, God was also blessing everything we set our hand to, and the more diligent we were in setting our hands to it, the more He would bless it!

Diligence and God's Wisdom Brought a Turnaround

Things started to improve. It didn't seem rapid at the time since we were working long, hard hours at it, but the fact is that it only took a little over a year to turn our business around. By November of 1977, only fifteen months after we were married, we had paid off all of our debts and the dress shop was making money again! It was around this time that Judy felt that God was leading us to sell it. I thought she was crazy! We had just started making money. Then, over the next two months, we lost $6,000, so I was suddenly convinced she was right! So, in February of 1978, we sold the shop for $30,000, and gave $10,000 of it to her mother for her part in the shop.

Buying Our First Home

That same year we had been living in a little rental house in Alvin and the city decided that it needed to build a street that would go right through the property it was on. We bought the house (without the land, of course) for practically nothing and then used the money from the dress shop to buy twelve acres out in the country. We moved the house onto the twelve acres and got it all set up. It was pretty wild, because we moved the house with everything in it: dishes, couches, bed, TV, everything! We paid about $1,800 an acre for the land, and bought the house and got it all set up for about $10,000, so all in all it cost about $30,000. That was a lot of money back in 1978, though it doesn't sound like so much today. But, we now owned our own home and the land it was on—and we hadn't borrowed a dime to buy it!

By October of that year we had completely moved onto the new land and were living in our new house. We'd had some pretty wild adventures along the way, like the time when we had a downpour before the workers finished putting the roof back on the house! We spent the whole night catching water in small plastic containers, pouring those into buckets, and dumping the water down the bathtub drain. Yet God had seen us through it all and we were able to stick to our plan—we paid cash for everything and didn't owe money on any of it!

We thought we were so incredibly blessed by what God was doing in our lives—and we were!—but it wasn't long before we began to realize that God had even more in store for us.

3

GOD HAS STOREHOUSES

**He gathers the waters of the sea together as a heap;
He lays up the deep in storehouses.**

PSALM 33:7 NASB

In the early 1980s I went out to lunch with a pastor friend. By
this time we had sold the little house and the twelve-acre plot of land
for a good profit which allowed us to move into a nicer home closer
to the church. Because of our personal storehouse, we were again
able to pay for it with cash. The church was also continuing to grow
and we were looking to move into new facilities soon because we
needed more room. God was helping us to grow as we obeyed Him.

If you have ever been to Texas, you know that we are famous for
our barbeque restaurants. The one that my friend and I had gone to
for lunch was old and rustic with heavy wooden tables and a wood-
en floor. As we sat there and talked about the things pastors talk
about, he told me about one of the messages he had preached recently at his church.

"Al," he said, "Let me ask you something: when you think of
wood, what do you think of?"

The question really caught me off guard. What was he talking about? "I don't really ever think of wood," I answered.

"No, no, no. Listen, let me ask you again in another way: if I ask you to picture *wood* in your head, what do you think of?"

Still a bit confused by what he was saying, I looked around the room for a moment and my eyes fell on one of the tables nearby. "Oh, I don't know. How about a wooden table?"

"Okay, that's good. But think about this now: when God thinks about *wood*, He would think of something like the redwood forests of the world, or the Amazon jungle. God doesn't think small like we do. He thinks big." Then he went on before I could respond, "When you think about *rock*, what do you think of?"

Again I looked around. I caught a view of the gravel in the parking lot outside, so I said, "I don't know, how about rocks on a driveway?"

"Okay," he accepted, "but when God thinks of rock, He thinks of something like the Rocky Mountains, the Himalayas, the Appalachians, or the Andes, because He is a God of abundance." Again, he went on, "When you think of *water*, what do you think of?"

Again, I wanted to say, "I don't think about water," but I knew he wouldn't accept that answer, so I looked around the room again. "How about a glass of water?"

"Well, to know what God thinks when He thinks of water, you would have to go to the oceans of the world—the Pacific, Atlantic, Indian, and all of them rolled into one—because our God is a God of more than enough."

Seeing Things from God's Perspective

Suddenly, with that picture in my mind, I got all excited on the inside. I knew what he was saying was true. God never did anything without creating more than He needed. He always had hundreds—thousands, millions—of times more than He needed in reserves. Yet if He knew that He could create anything He wanted, why didn't He just create enough to get by for the moment, and then create the rest to meet the need as it arose later?

Think about this for a moment:

- To hold the one planet on which He placed humanity, He created a universe with billions of solar systems, many of which hold planets of their own—why did He need so many extra?

- To feed Adam and Eve, He created a whole planet of food. Why so much? Why didn't He just wait for the generations to follow to come along and let more food-bearing plants grow as they were needed?

- If Adam and Eve had needed a drink, would they have needed much more than a stream? But God created enough water to cover seventy percent of the earth! Did He really need so much in reserves to take care of His children?

- According to Psalm 50, He owns all of the creatures of the forest and the cattle on a thousand hills—if He can create more any time He would like, wouldn't the cattle on ten hills, or even a hundred, have been enough?

Look for a moment at what Psalm 33 says about God's creation:

> The Lord loves righteousness and justice;
> the earth is full of his unfailing love.
>
> By the word of the Lord were the heavens made,
> their starry host by the breath of his mouth.
>
> *He gathers the waters of the sea into jars;*
> *he puts the deep into storehouses.*
>
> Let all the earth fear the Lord;
> let all the people of the world revere him.
>
> For he spoke, and it came to be;
> he commanded, and it stood firm.
>
> PSALM 33:5-9 NIV (*italics added*)

God created so much water that He needed to put some of it into the storehouses of the deep to hold it in reserve. Would He ever need all that water? Probably not, because He could always make more. Then why all of the extra?

The Nature of God

Suddenly, I began to see that was just His nature—He is a God of extra, a God of reserves, a God of storehouses. He always has more than He needs no matter what happens. Even in the finite sense of what is on earth, He would never run out and we will never run out of what we need. God doesn't have a scarcity mentality!

Let me give you an example of what I mean. There are lots of people worried today that we will soon run out of fossil fuels to heat our homes and power our cars—if you look at the statistics, this is a reasonable concern. Yet, at the same time, technologies are already being developed to replace those fuels with hydrogen or solar power. In other words, as humanity needs it, God will reveal to us new technologies to meet our needs until He is ready to come back for us. Could Adam and Eve ever have imagined that one day the earth would hold more than six billion people? And yet, somehow, we are surviving. Despite the desperate needs in many areas of the world, if you were to take all the wealth and food in the world and divide it up, everyone would have more than enough. Why? *Because God created vast storehouses of "extra" when He created the earth.*

Don't Box Yourself In

People with scarcity mentalities tend to be more limited by what they see inside of the box, rather than coming up with answers outside of the box. As with the energy example above, a scarcity mentality only sees our ever-decreasing supply of fossil fuels and panics, screaming "Conservation! Conservation! Conservation! Look at your waste!" While a person with an abundance mentality would see that there are other answers to the energy problem and throw their efforts into being a part of the solution as well as part of conservation. Chances are that those investing their energies in new sources of power will find the answers we need for the future and be the big financial winners in the long run!

People with a scarcity mentality tend to either hoard or spend. Either they think there is not enough, so they sock away what they have in order to hoard it for themselves (the Ebenezer Scrooges of the world); or, on the other extreme, they spend everything that comes into their hands, and more, because they feel that if they don't get what they want *right now*, they never will. They buy on impulse and credit to get what they want *now*. They fill their homes with stuff—some of which wears out even before it has been paid for—and then they have to rent storage units to hold the stuff that won't fit in their homes! They have their *stuff*, but have no financial reserves. Then they end up in a cycle of debt and lack that further feeds their scarcity mentality and leads to more and more troubles.

Have an Attitude of Abundance

Yet an abundance mentality can save and wait. It has the patience and self-control to find a cheaper alternative or wait on God for a better answer. An abundance mentality can put money away as a foundation for later. Though it is not being saved for any specific reason—like buying a specific car, house, or sofa—it is being saved as a foundation for whatever God wants you to do in the future. It's insurance that you'll be able to fulfill God's plans for your life when He reveals them to you. It can be saved because *there is enough to go around*. It can be shared with others because more can be gathered from the abundance that's out there to receive. This mentality builds up reserves and encourages others to do the same because of the stability and peace that comes from having more than enough. This abundance mentality also looks outside of the box and not only builds up reserves on earth, but stores up treasures in heaven. It is a mentality that says there is more than enough, so in every situation I will be a blessing to others and not a drain on them.

I realized this even further as I began to hear about how other churches raised money for their needs. These were not for frivolous things, but for good projects. They would come to their congregations and say something like, "After last week's thunderstorm, we found some damage to the roof over the nursery. We need $3,000 to fix that before another big storm comes and soaks all of our kids! So we are going to pass the offering plates again after you give your tithe to start raising money to fix it." Then a month or so later, "Well, summer will soon be here, and we need to have some repairs made on the air conditioning, so we need to raise an extra $5,000 this week. Please write a second check for that and label it 'For the new air conditioner.'" Then a few weeks later, "We wanted to help some kids go to church camp this summer who can't afford to pay their own way. If you would like to help defer the costs for this, please check the 'Other' box on your offering envelopes and write in 'Camp Scholarships.'"

As I saw this over and over again, I started thinking, *If God needed $5,000 for some project He wanted to do, where would He get it?*

Well, I answered myself, *He would get it from Himself.*

Then if He got it from Himself, how much would He have left?

He would still have an infinite supply left, because He has enormous reserves and can create more as He needs it!

Some Businesses Have Storehouses

But this wasn't all of it. I then began to see in the newspapers how large companies would buy out other large companies for millions, hundred of millions, or even billions of dollars. How did they have the money to do such things?

There was only one answer. Because they had large storehouses filled with money (or partnered with banks that did), it allowed them to step in and buy others out when they were in need, and by doing so, would make even more money than they were making before. I began to see why the rich do get richer and why the poor get poorer. But I also saw that having a storehouse for the church and for ourselves allowed God to put His provision into the hands of His children, rather than people who have no love nor fear of God.

Even while all of this was happening, little did I know of the magnitude of God's purposes for teaching me these lessons. God was preparing me for even more. Up to that point, I thought I had discovered something pretty special in the Storehouse Principle, but I didn't have any idea about the scope of it yet. As God was showing me these things, He was preparing to take it to an even greater level. He was preparing me for the blessing that was to start happening next.

4

THE STOREHOUSE BLESSING

Oh, the joys of those
who do not follow the advice of the wicked,
or stand around with sinners,
or join in with scoffers.

But they delight in doing everything the LORD wants;
day and night they think about his law.

They are like trees planted along the riverbank,
bearing fruit each season without fail.
Their leaves never wither,
and in all they do, they prosper.

PSALM 1:1-3 NLT

Sometime later in the early 1980s, while I was watching the church prosper and grow and seeing God bless my family, a man by the name of Carlos Ortiz came to visit me. I had never met him before; he just came to me out of the blue.

As Carlos and I sat together in my office, he began, "Did you know that they are going to grant a construction permit for a television station in Alvin?"

"Oh, really?" I said.

"Yes," he went on. "And you know what? I specialize in filling out the forms to apply for those permits. Because the Federal Communication Commission (FCC) regulates all of this so closely, the forms for these applications are very complicated and you have to know your stuff to fill them out. You have to really know what you are doing if you want to get yours accepted out of all those who file."

Again, I didn't know what to say except, "Oh, really?"

He went on: "Let me get to the point. I am really, really good at this kind of thing, and I think God wants me fill out this paperwork so that you can get the permit to build this television station. Can I do the paperwork for you to get the permit?"

I was a little shocked, of course, and thought he was at least a little crazy, but since God had been opening my mind up to bigger things I thought, *Why not? At least it would be a good learning experience, and it won't cost me anything!* So I told him, "Do whatever you think you should. I don't have the money to build something like that, but if you feel God is telling you to do it, then do whatever He tells you!"

He said that he would fill out the application, and left my office and got started soon after that.

Getting into the Television Business

As things developed, I started learning a good deal about television stations and the television industry, in general. We submitted our paperwork and there were soon five or six other groups who had also submitted their paperwork to get the permit. The FCC had set a deadline for filing the permits, and on the day before the deadline, a huge company from New York submitted its application. When that happened, all of the other applicants withdrew their applications because they didn't want to compete with this firm—it was too large and powerful and they knew they couldn't win against them.

However, I had never really planned on getting our application accepted anyway, and I wanted to wait and see what would happen. As it turned out, Carlos had done a great job of setting up the company and preparing the application. He had pulled together people from various cultures and backgrounds to be on our board so that we had the diversity that government agencies favor and a wide range of experience to pull from. So when it came time for the applications to go before an FCC judge for the ruling, it was just the New York outfit and us. I had no idea what I was doing, but thanks to the work that Carlos had done, we were still very much in the running to get the permit.

Preparation Meets Opportunity

As it turned out, we had such a good chance of getting the station that the big New York firm got nervous. I knew that because one of their executives called me. They wanted me to withdraw our application and offered to pay me to do so. He asked me, "What can we give you to get you out of this deal?" I told the man that I would think about it and get back to him.

So I contacted some friends to see what I should do. One friend from Washington, D.C. who knew about such things advised me, "If they want the station badly enough, and you get the permit, they will take you to court and force you out of the running over time. If you win in court, they will keep appealing it until you don't have a dime left to fight back. They have so much money, they will gladly take the losses of the court proceedings until you are broke and have to drop out and settle with them. But, you know what? Right now, you are still in the driver's seat."

"Okay," I responded, "so what should I do?"

"If I were you, I would make the deal with them now, up front, rather than later when you are out of money, and then get out. If you do it now, you can ask for whatever you want. If you do it later, you will have to take whatever terms they are willing to give you."

That made sense to me, especially since if we got the permit, I really didn't have the money to build the station anyway! So I thought and prayed about what I would ask for to withdraw our application. When the answer came, it must have been from God, because the way it turned out was better than anything I could have ever thought of on my own!

An Incredible Blessing

A few days later, I called the executive back and told him, "If you pay me $50,000 in cash, and give me a contract for two hours of air-time every Sunday morning from 8:00 to 10:00 AM for four years, and get it ruled on and signed off by an FCC judge, I will withdraw our application. I don't want you to just buy me out and give me a contract, though. I want it ratified by an FCC judge." I didn't fully understand at the time why I was being so adamant about having our agreement ratified by the FCC, but that was just what was in my heart, so I obeyed it.

The executive from New York didn't even make a counteroffer. He agreed to my terms over the phone. I never met with anyone in person, and never left Alvin, but soon had a check for $50,000 and a contract for two hours of airtime every Sunday for the next four years to preach the gospel on TV! I put the $50,000 in the church storehouse, we got some used camera equipment from Lakewood Church using some of the money from the church's general expenses account, and started broadcasting every Sunday to the Houston area.

As it turned out, Carlos never made a dime on the deal either—he donated all of his time and effort because he felt it was what God had wanted him to do. He just popped in, did the work, and popped out. And he didn't even go to our church! You don't meet many people like that today, I am sorry to say. I never even heard from or about him again until he died a few years ago. He was an incredible blessing to us!

The Next Step

Yet God was still not done with our storehouse blessing. About six months later, a limousine pulled up in front of the church and four men wearing the most expensive-looking pinstriped suits I had ever seen in my life came into the church and asked if I had time to meet with them. When I agreed, they came into my office. I shook hands with them all and asked them to sit down. They informed me that they represented the New York company that owned the local channel and they wanted to ask me something. I agreed to listen, so one of the men leaned forward and began, "Pastor Jandl, I will be honest with you. We are going to sell the TV station here in Alvin. In the last six months we have lost $15 million on it, and it doesn't look to be getting any better very soon. We are either going to file bankruptcy on it or sell it. We would rather sell it, and we even have a buyer for it, but we can't sell it to them with you on the air. They don't want any local broadcasting, so we have to get you to agree to go off before they will buy it."

As we continued to talk about this, I began to realize that I had tripped over something very significant in requiring our agreement to be ratified by an FCC judge. They informed me that they could cancel their other contracts for movies, etc., and fight out their breach of contracts in court and pay only part of what they owed to square things up, but because an FCC judge had ratified their agreement with me, they couldn't touch me with a ten-foot pole! They had to honor their agreement with me or get me to agree to let them out of the deal! So the man asked me, "Sir, if you don't graciously agree to go off the air, we have no choice but to file bankruptcy. So, would you agree to give up your air time so that we can sell the station?"

Leaning Back on God's Wisdom

Can you imagine? There I was, surrounded by all of these men in expensive suits putting pressure on me, but I didn't lose my composure. I knew that if the agreement was going to be a win-win proposition for both parties, I should get something in compensation for the time that the church was giving up, so I asked him, "Well, how much are you offering me to void our contract?"

They were shocked. One of the men said, "We didn't plan to offer you anything! You're a preacher, and we're in trouble, and we thought you would just be good and help us!"

"Well, I am trying to be good," I replied. "I just don't think that the church should give up its airtime for nothing. I think we should get something for this."

They looked at each other for a moment, and then one of them said, "We would be willing to give you $35,000."

I was a little shocked at them offering so much in such a short amount of time, but I was also determined to get more advice before I agreed to anything, so I told them, "Well, give me a few days to think that over, and I'll let you know." We all shook hands again, and they left.

In a Multitude of Counselors There Is Safety

However, I didn't just think about it. I called all of the television stations I could find in the phone book, and asked them how much it would be for three and a half years of airtime on their stations for an 8:00 to 10:00 A.M. block every Sunday morning. The amounts were in the millions of dollars. So I eventually called the New York executives back and offered, "If you will give me $300,000, I will get off the air." Out of that, we finally settled on $230,000. I agreed to that amount on the condition that the money would be in my bank account in the next twenty-four hours and they had the FCC judge approve the agreement again. They said that they would see that both of these things happened.

I remember that was on a Tuesday. They wired the money into the church's storehouse account the next day, which was of course a Wednesday. Now, from the original $1,000 I had deposited into the account several years before, we had almost $300,000 in the church's storehouse! We had that $230,000, plus the $50,000 from the initial deal on the TV station, plus the original $1,000, plus all the other deposits we had been making regularly and faithfully into that account over the years.

But God Still Had More

On the very next day, Thursday morning of that same week, I received a telephone call from someone saying he represented a certain network. The man informed me that they were the ones who had bought the channel and taken me off the air.

"Oh," I said, "I knew someone had bought the station, but I didn't know it was you guys."

"Yes, it was us," he responded, "but in reviewing the situation, I was asked to call you and make a request. You see, we just lost a major lawsuit in Ohio because any time you own a local station, you have to have local broadcasting on it. At the moment, we don't know of any local programming down there but you. Would you be willing to stay on the air for a while?"

This time I didn't have to think or pray about it. I almost laughed out loud over the phone, but I controlled myself and simply said, "Sure, we'll stay on." So in the end we agreed to go back on the air for an hour every Sunday morning. That allowed us to continue our outreach to the local community and the church continued to prosper and grow. And still God wasn't done.

God's Blessings and Wisdom Have Continued to Flow

It wasn't too long afterwards that we built the 2,500-seat auditorium where we still hold our services today. The odd thing about it was that although I had first considered using the money in the storehouse to pay for part of the building, every time we finished a new phase of the building and I needed to make a payment, we had enough to cover it from the general funds of the church. We never had any special fundraisers or building drives, either. We just started building, and when we needed to make a payment, the money was there to cover it.

I have to be honest with you: I don't have that kind of wisdom all by myself. I believe that it is part of the blessing from the second part of Deuteronomy 28:8: when you have a storehouse, God will also command a blessing on everything you set your hand to. I know this is true, because it has not just happened to us. God has done similar things for others who have heard this testimony from me and who have applied the Storehouse Principle in their lives. If you will study and learn how to apply this principle in your life, you can put yourself in a place to be used by God to reach your community and your world as you never have before!

5

SEEING AFAR OFF

**But he that lacketh these things is blind,
and cannot see afar off.**

2 PETER 1:9

When the domed sanctuary of Living Stones Church was just finished in the mid 1980s, it seemed like a time to settle in and expect many years of growth and prosperity. Everything was paid for and the ministry lacked for nothing. The future seemed clear and simple: the church "had arrived" and had everything it would ever need.

It was about this time that my wife and I became interested in buying some land for the construction of a new home. The land belonged to a couple in California, and after we had contacted them they flew to Alvin for a visit. After negotiating a price for the property, the owner and I stood looking out the front windows of the church lobby. It was at this point that the man asked me a question that completely changed the focus for our future and the future of our church.

It was really a simple question. "Are you going to buy that land across the street for your church?" he asked. The property he referred to was pasture land at that time.

"Oh, no sir. We'll never need that," I told him.

"Oh, I see," he answered. "So, you're the selfish type then."

"Excuse me?" I was startled and couldn't believe my ears. What was he trying to say?

The man continued, "What I meant to say is you are only thinking about yourself and what your church needs while *you* are still the pastor here. What is going to happen a hundred years from now when the church wants to expand and there is no land available?"

His comments struck pretty hard. No one was looking twenty years down the road—in fact, we were all pretty content with what had already been accomplished. But the fact of the matter was that God had a lot more in store for Living Stones than to just erect a new church building. In fact, Living Stones was just getting started!

Eventually Living Stones bought twenty acres across the street from the church building, and that land is where Victory Camp sits today.

Another Word of Wisdom

As some of the first dormitories were going up for Victory Camp, God used another man, a man from Australia, to change my perspectives again. He said that if what a person does for God isn't around a hundred years after that person has died, then that person hasn't really done anything at all.

So we went back to the drawing board. Instead of building the dormitories out of metal, we switched to brick. The plan was for those buildings to be a blessing to several generations of kids, not just a couple of generations.

God was teaching me to look "afar off," and not just think for today. If Christians are going to change the world, we need to learn to think the same way about our futures, the futures of our families, and the impact our churches will have in the times to come.

He Is the God of Yesterday, Today, and Tomorrow

If Living Stones Church hadn't bought that land all those years ago, Victory Camp would never have happened. That is why Living Stones Church now owns over 280 acres in Alvin. There are no specific plans for all of that land at the present time, but it will be there for the church to use to fulfill its future dreams.

In 1 Chronicles 22, David prepared for the next generation in his time.

> **And David prepared iron in abundance for the nails for the doors of the gates, and for the joinings; and brass in abundance without weight; Also cedar trees in abundance: for the Sidonians and they of Tyre brought much cedar wood to David. And David said, Solomon my son is young and tender, and the house that is to be built for the LORD must be exceedingly magnificent, of fame and of glory throughout all countries: I will therefore now make preparation for it. So David prepared abundantly before his death.**
>
> 1 CHRONICLES 22:3-5

David wasn't thinking just about himself. God had told him he would not be allowed to build the Temple. But he did not let that deter him. He knew that one day the Temple would be built, so he was going to prepare for it. He was seeing afar off and thinking about what he could do today to help someone else tomorrow. He never got to see the magnificence of this house of the Lord, but he knew that it would bless the next generation.

It was this attitude of seeing "afar off" that drove him to prepare so much for the building of this house. David was not only a man after God's own heart, but also a man of vision and faith. He was willing to invest today for what others would reap tomorrow. Too often, we only see and live for the present. But, if you live by the Storehouse Principle, your vision will move beyond the present and look to the future. It is this principle that prepared for Victory Camp before it was even imagined, and why Living Stones has a camp to reach youth, a school, and a day-care facility, all of which are designed to minister to the next generation upon a foundation that is built today.

Joseph, one of the twelve sons of Jacob, also prepared for the future. For seven years he stored up food for a famine that was about to come to the region where he lived.

> **Have them gather all the food and grain of these good
> years into the royal storehouses, and store it away
> so there will be food in the cities. That way there will be
> enough to eat when the seven years of famine come.**

**Otherwise disaster will surely strike the land,
and all the people will die."**

**Joseph's suggestions were well received by Pharaoh
and his advisers.**

GENESIS 41:35-37 NIV

Because of his wisdom and ability to see afar off, Joseph built storehouses and saved the abundance of the present for the scarcity that would come in the future. He not only saved his own natural family, but in doing so he also secured the future of Israel as a nation because his family was the foundation for that great nation. Not only that, but he also secured the future of Egypt, which is where he lived at the time of the famine. No wonder Pharaoh (the ruler of Egypt) and all his servants "liked" the idea.

So, what about you? Do you have a storehouse for your kids' college education or for your retirement? Are you looking down the road financially? Or do you have to have the newest model car or the latest high-tech toy *today*? Do you always take the money you get from a raise and use it to buy something new rather than investing it for the future? Are you blinded by trying to keep up with what your neighbors have? It could be that spending what you have in the present will cause you to miss golden opportunities in the future. As Edwin Louis Cole once said, "We sow to the future and reap from the past."

What Do You Have "Planted" for Your Future?

In some nations around the world many people develop savings that are equal to *years* of their current annual salaries for no other purpose than to have that money set aside as a back-up. This does not even include the money they have set aside for their children's college, their own retirement, and even for providing for their children's first home when they marry. Meanwhile, the average American has no more than two months salary in the bank at any one time and often carries more than that in credit card debt alone.

Proverbs 13:22 says, "A good man leaves an inheritance for his children's children." What do you have that is saved and invested for your grandchildren to inherit?

God wants to expand His kingdom on earth today, and that kingdom includes both the children of God who embrace Him now and also those who will be reached with the Gospel in the future. A storehouse is a foundation upon which we can establish that kingdom. And it is not just for church congregations and organizations; God wants to establish His kingdom in our personal lives and in the lives of our family members as well.

It is time to stop simply thinking about it and to start building the future by putting the Storehouse Principle to work in your life today.

6

THE JOSEPH PRINCIPLE

**Then turning to the others standing nearby,
the king ordered, "Take the money from this servant,
and give it to the one who earned the most."**

**"But, master," they said, "that servant has
enough already!"**

**"Yes," the king replied, "but to those who use well
what they are given, even more will be given.
But from those who are unfaithful, even what little
they have will be taken away."**

LUKE 19:24-26 NLT

As we have already seen, the concept of having storehouses—or barns or treasuries as they are called in other parts of the Bible—is not something unique to Deuteronomy 28:8. We don't have to search long to find that David had a storehouse to collect materials for the Temple and that he also commissioned storehouses to be built throughout Israel in case of famine or war.[1] Nehemiah had storehouses to stockpile wealth and materials to rebuild Jerusalem

---

[1] See 1 Chronicles 27:25.

and the temple.[2] Jewish farmers kept extra in their storehouses in case there might be a crop failure or pestilence. Hezekiah had "heaps" laid up into the storehouses of the temple[3] and "prospered in all his works".[4] And in the early days of church history, Macedonian Christians "stored" up their offerings for Christians in Jerusalem so they could send resources to help them in time of need.[5]

Jesus' parable of the ten virgins also speaks of the wisdom of having reserves or storehouses. In this parable, according to Jewish custom, ten virgins were awaiting the appearance of a certain bridegroom during the night. After his arrival, they were to enter the place where the wedding feast was being held, along with him. The ten virgins didn't know the exact time when the bridegroom would arrive, so they didn't know how much oil would be needed to keep their lamps burning. Five of the virgins brought along extra oil with them in case they began to run out of oil for their lamps. The other five did not. At some point, the oil in their lamps did begin to run out, and those without reserves had to leave their posts in order to buy replacement oil. The bridegroom showed up while the five were away buying oil, and the five who had brought an abundance got into the wedding feast; the five without reserves did not.[6]

---

[2] See Nehemiah 7:70-72; 13:12-13.
[3] See 2 Chronicles 31:6-10.
[4] See 2 Chronicles 32:27-30.
[5] See 1 Corinthians 16:1-2.
[6] See Matthew 25:1-13.

All of these people began saving in their storehouses when they had little or nothing, and they prospered as God commanded a blessing on them in their storehouses. It is one thing to have a storehouse, but another to see it multiplied through wise investment. Those who are faithful with what they have will have an opportunity to turn it into more. This is another aspect of the Storehouse Principle which I will call the "Joseph Principle."

Joseph's Storehouses

Many people think that it was Joseph's interpretation of Pharaoh's dream that got him out of prison and got him promoted to the second highest position in the nation of Egypt in a day, but that is not entirely true. Actually, it was the wisdom that he shared *after* his interpretation of Pharaoh's dream that got him the promotion. After Joseph told Pharaoh of seven years of plenty that would be followed by seven years of severe famine, as shown to him in his dream, he added these words of advice:

> **"Now therefore, let Pharaoh select a discerning and wise man, . . . and let him appoint officers over the land, to collect one-fifth of the produce of the land of Egypt in the seven plentiful years. . . . That food shall be as a reserve for the land for the seven years of famine which shall be in the land of Egypt, that the land may not perish during the famine."**

> **GENESIS 41:33-34,36 NJKV**

Through this encounter, Pharaoh recognized Joseph to be both wise and filled with the Spirit of God. Did there exist a better person in all the land of Egypt to put this plan into action? So it was on that day that Joseph traded prison rags for robes of royalty—all because he walked closely with God and understood the Storehouse Principle.

Now it is one thing to know that Joseph put the Storehouse Principle into action and saved both Egypt and Israel in the process, but it's also important to appreciate how Joseph managed the wealth of Egypt during the seven years of plenty. Genesis 47:13-20 tells us the results of his entrepreneurship. In the seven years of famine, Joseph used the storehouses he had built to obtain for Pharaoh *all* of the money in Egypt, plus *all* of the land and livestock. Finally, even *all* of the people sold themselves into slavery to Pharaoh so that they farmed the land for him and paid Pharaoh proceeds from the sale of their crops. Everything that could be bought and sold in the land of Egypt (except what belonged to the priests) now belonged to Pharaoh, and all of the people now worked for him, farming their lands and tending their livestock, but giving Pharaoh one fifth of all their increase every year.

The Joseph Principle in Action

Now think about this for a moment: in one fourteen-year period, because of careful and diligent savings during seven prosperous years, Joseph was able to buy *everything* that could be bought in the land of Egypt over the next seven years of economic recession.

You don't have to read too many books on financial management and the majority of America's millionaires to find out that this same principle has helped many of them create their financial independence: save in prosperous times when others are spending frivolously, then when the economy stumbles, buy at reduced prices when others are desperate to sell because they need the cash.

The Joseph Principle is thus built on three key truths:

- there are cycles of prosperity and recession in every economy;

- during times of prosperity, surpluses should be saved and not consumed; and

- in times of recession, that surplus can be multiplied into more wealth as it is used to help meet the needs of others.

There Will Always Be Economic Cycles

One of the things that the United States seemed to forget during the 1990s (and actually during the 1920s as well, if you study history) is that the economy, like the weather, comes in seasons and cycles. The 1990s and the 1920s were the most prosperous decades in the history of the world, and while economists warned that it couldn't last forever, everyone seemed willing to risk everything to take advantage of the climbing stock market that defied the limits of all previous periods of financial success and the ready availability of credit. During the 1990s, mutual funds were exploding and no analyst seemed to be able to make bad choices as the overall market for investments kept breaking its own records. Yet, despite everyone's optimism and despite surviving the Y2K scare, the market took a nosedive in the early 2000s. Many of those who had ridden their roller coasters to the top also rode them to the bottom. As of this writing, it seems that every month a new record is set for the number of bankruptcy filings. Although the market now seems to be turning around again, events, from the attacks of September 11th to the corporate accounting scandals of Enron, WorldCom and others, to the war in Iraq, have created huge questions about the health of the U.S. economy. Although, during the 1990s, many statistics seemed to indicate that the economic boom would never end, the truth has turned out otherwise: The economy will always have ups and downs.

Economic cycles are inevitable, though hopefully not as severe as the two seven-year cycles that Joseph saw in his lifetime. Just as there is a time to plant and a time to harvest, there is a time to put more into our storehouses and a time where we may need to put in less. There will also be a time to give out of our storehouses and a time to replenish them, or we may do a combination of the two. There is also a time to invest our savings conservatively, and a time God may instruct us to use it to build wealth more aggressively. Just as Solomon said in Ecclesiastes:

> To everything there is a season,
> A time for every purpose under heaven: . . .
>
> A time to plant, And a time to pluck what is planted; . . .
>
> A time to break down, And a time to build up; . . .
>
> A time to gain, And a time to lose;
> A time to keep, And a time to throw away.

ECCLESIASTES 3:1-3,6 NJKV

Or, as Jesus said:

> "He makes His sun rise on the evil and on the good, and
> sends rain on the just and on the unjust. . . .
>
> "Therefore whoever hears these sayings of Mine, and does
> them, I will liken him to a wise man who built his house
> on the rock: and the rain descended, the floods came, and
> the winds blew and beat on that house; and it did not fall,
> for it was founded on the rock.
>
> "But everyone who hears these sayings of Mine, and does
> not do them, will be like a foolish man who built his
> house on the sand: and the rain descended, the floods
> came, and the winds blew and beat on that house; and it
> fell. And great was its fall."

MATTHEW 5:45; 7:24-27 NKJV

In other words, cycles of nature and circumstances don't only happen to bad people, they happen to everyone. Those who are wisely prepared for them are the ones who "weather" the storms. Those who build their houses—in the financial realm as well as in the other areas of our lives—firmly on the Word of God and His principles will not only survive these storms but will often be stronger afterwards. The Bible warns us again and again that times of trial, persecution, and temptation will be with us always as long as we are here on this earth, but it also tells us that if we will be strong in Christ that we will overcome trials, withstand persecution, and be able to resist temptation. The keys to the difference between smooth sailing through the storms and shipwreck are in obeying God's Word, living by His principles, abiding firmly in Him, and following His individual guidance to each of us. In the financial realm, those who have storehouses can insulate themselves from the effects of economic declines because their reserves hedge them against downturns and, during times of recession, they can actually be in position to make money rather than to lose it.

Having a Storehouse Can Turn
Economic Downturn into Times of Increase

This not only happens as the overall economy of a nation goes through cycles, but also as individuals experience personal economic cycles. Opportunity often knocks on the door of those who have storehouses. In the years since Living Stones built its new sanctuary in the mid 1980s, I have been presented with various "deals" by people who needed cash right away. Once, a lawyer approached with an offer to sell me $479,000 worth of land for $26,000. Another man offered to sell a Rolls Royce for $12,000. One financially strapped person offered to sell a house for $250,000 although it had cost $3,000,000 to build it! Others have approached with offers to sell jewelry and other items. Although I was financially able to take advantage of all of these opportunities, for various reasons I declined—but it has not been for lack of opportunity. The deals didn't feel right at the time, so I let them pass.

The church and I have, however, taken advantage of numerous other opportunities. All of the beautiful executive desks that are in the church offices today were bought for pennies on the dollar from a real estate agency that was consolidating because of the Texas oil slump of the mid 1980s. All of the land the church owns was bought for far below market value. Patience, wisdom, self-control, and the ability to pay cash have brought some incredible additional blessings over the years.

One such opportunity came shortly after the church received the $230,000 for getting off of the TV station. Because interest rates were so high at the time, I invested the $300,000 that was in the church's storehouse account in a certificate of deposit at a local bank at about a fourteen percent interest rate for a five-year term. Shortly after that the bottom dropped out of the Texas oil market. The bank came to me and asked if I would take the money out of the certificate of deposit. Of course, since the church was benefiting from it and there wasn't a better deal to be found elsewhere, I refused. Then the bank asked if I would at least be willing to borrow some money instead. As it worked out, the church was able to borrow money from the bank at about a four percent interest rate when the going rate was much higher. The church used that money for its other projects while the $300,000 sat in the bank drawing interest. As it says in Deuteronomy 28:6, we were blessed going in and blessed going out!

By the grace of God, the stability of the storehouses at Living Stones has also helped the church to create, out of its regular cash flow, Living Stones Christian School (a fully-accredited K-12 school)—which is adding a new gymnasium as this book is being written. It has also helped to start Precious Stones Day Care and build Victory Camp. It has helped to expand Victory Camp each year. At the present time, the camp has dormitories for up to 430 overnight guests, a cafeteria that seats 500, a 700-seat meeting hall, a junior-Olympic-sized swimming pool, a hotel-quality lodge for guests, water slides, a basketball pavilion, a ropes and obstacle course, a go-kart track, a volleyball pit, a lake stocked with fish, paddle boats, two railroad cabooses that serve as ice cream shops, and a narrow-gauge train on its campus—all dedicated to help kids learn about God and to reach people in the Alvin area with the love of God. This past year the church added a pizza parlor that can be used for camp-related activities as well as for special church events. All of these activities, as well as other various outreach programs of the ministry, are possible because Living Stones has storehouses.

This happens every day in the business world, too. Businesses that have storehouses often buy other companies at very favorable prices. These transactions can involve large sums of money. How does this happen? Not by accident. When owners of a company, for one reason or another, decide to sell their business they typically want to deal with a financially strong buyer that has enough cash or borrowing ability to carry out the deal. That's what makes it a "win-win" situation for both parties. The "storehouse-oriented" business is able to buy the other company and often does a better job of running it, producing new profits for its owners.

In the church, in our personal lives, in the business world—"storehouse people" are in position to take advantage of the opportunities that God brings across our paths.

The Kingdom of God Needs More Josephs

When Christians follow God's principles of financial wisdom and live for the future and eternity rather than just living for today, God can lead us into the abundant life Jesus told us about in John 10:10. Now, money is definitely not all there is to life, but you have to admit that life is a lot easier if money is not a major source of concern for us. If we are willing to plug into God's wisdom, then we can have more than enough to meet our personal needs as well as expand the kingdom of God in the lives of ourselves, our families, our communities and our world.

Jesus echoed the Joseph principle in the parables of the talents (Matthew 25:14-30) and the pounds (Luke 19:12-17). Those who were wisest and multiplied their Lord's kingdom were trusted with more. Those who were foolish had even the little they were originally given taken away and given to the wiser stewards. Not only did these parables say that the wise would have more resources, but also that they would have more authority in the kingdom. We have too often made the mistake in thinking that seeking temporal wealth and spiritual wealth are mutually exclusive—that if you have one, you can't have the other—but Jesus' teaching said something quite different than that. He taught that money, in its proper place as a servant, can be an aid in establishing God's kingdom.

What God needs is a people who will rise up to be faithful in both natural and spiritual wealth. He needs people who are willing and obedient in both realms so that He can further establish His kingdom and covenant on the earth. In order to do that, though, we have to be faithful in what we have today, and not what we only hope to have someday.

Now that we've looked at how some giant corporations and the powerful nation of ancient Egypt utilized the storehouse principle, let's set our sights on something much, much smaller. The ant.

7

EVEN THE ANT HAS A STOREHOUSE

Go to the ant, you sluggard!
Consider her ways and be wise.

PROVERBS 6:6 NKJV

Why did God choose the ant? Why didn't God say, "Go to the elephant," "Go look at the lion," "Go look at the eagle," or "Go look at a bear, or a bull"? With any of these there would have been a show of strength, force, power, and beauty. Economists refer to the stock market as a bull or bear market because we think of bulls and bears as aggressive animals. When you visit the home offices of a major firm, you commonly see a statue of an animal that symbolizes their corporate vision—typically it's a huge eagle or a lion, or even an antelope, a deer, or an elk. Have you ever walked into an office and seen the statue of an ant there? Probably, none of us has ever seen a statue of an ant sitting on the desk of an important businessman. Most of us think of ants as pests. Have you ever had sugar ants in your house? If you do, you don't want to watch them, but you'll do everything you can to get rid of them. Or have you ever had an encounter with stinging red ants? If you have, you will never forget it!

Yet, in showing us how to get things accomplished in our lives, God has told us to observe the ant, not these other imposing, elegant animals. He says, "Go look at the ant and then consider what she is doing." There must be something very important to look at in the ant's life that He wants us to notice.

Proverbs 6:6 tells us to do three things. First of all it tells us to "*go to the ant*." In other words, find a colony of ants and watch them. Pay attention to what each ant is doing. Then the verse tells us to "*consider her ways*." Think about the way ants live, what they do and why. Finally, this verse states, "*be wise*." In other words, there are great lessons of wisdom to be learned from studying and understanding an ant's life. So what is it that God really wants us to learn from the ant?

Ants Are Diligent and Self-Directed

By what principles do ants live? Proverbs 6:7-8 tells us ants have "no captain, overseer or ruler," yet they gather their food during the harvest and it lasts them until the next summer. Ants produce and gather, preparing for the future, storing up against the winter or calamity. The ant is not just thinking about today, she's preparing for tomorrow.

Do you remember the old fable about the ant and the grasshopper? The ant works hard all year long to store up for the winter, while the grasshopper plays and gathers nothing. When winter hits and the snows fall, the grasshopper begins to starve and must go to the ants to beg in order to survive. Meanwhile, the ants are warm, safe, and secure—and they have plenty to help the grasshopper out in his need.

Notice again, God said to go to the ant—not the grasshopper.

In order for the ant to gather and prepare for the future, she must have a storehouse. We believe God is teaching us that if we are wise like the ant, we will have a storehouse for the "winter" seasons of life. Then, as springtime begins, the ant is still living off her storehouse, but she also begins again to immediately gather to rebuild and strengthen her storehouse for the next winter. The ant never stops working on her storehouse, and always has more than enough.

For us, "winter" could mean a number of different things. It could mean an unexpected change in our careers, an accident, an economic slump, or any number of "emergencies" or "storms" that come into our lives. Some of these may even be good things, or seasons that we can plan for, like our children going to college, buying a new home or car, starting our own businesses, or even retiring. Ants don't live in denial, consuming all they have today, for today, and believing that "winter" will never come; grasshoppers, however, do.

Even if an ant can only put one grain at a time into her storehouses, she still does it. Her storehouses are also in a large network of underground tunnels (she is diversified so that if one is destroyed by a storm, the others will still be intact); and her storehouses have different purposes (some are to take care of the young, others to make it through the winter, others set aside provisions in case winter is longer then expected, etc.). Ants work hard to take care of themselves and their colony and don't expect anyone else to take care of them.

Indeed, there is a great deal we can learn from seeing what ants do with their surpluses and how diligently they manage them and work to make sure they have more than enough.

Our Storehouses Are Not Only for Us

The ant not only has a storehouse for herself, but also for others. Bears store up food in their own bodies for themselves, and then sleep through the winter. Likewise, camels store up water in themselves so they can travel through the desert. Almost all other animals you can think of store up food in some way, but only for themselves. A storehouse, however, should not just be a source of blessing for ourselves and the members of our immediate families, but also a resource of blessing to touch others. God blesses us so that we can be a blessing.

There has been a great deal of debate and criticism in the church in recent years on the subject of Bible prosperity. It is true that some have misappropriated true prosperity for selfish purposes, but that doesn't change the fact that God wants to bless His children. It is our hope that through understanding what the Bible says about money and the Storehouse Principle that you will get an accurate perspective on what real prosperity is. Some people have become so upset about the subject that they say, "I don't believe in prosperity, and I don't like to hear about prosperity." But, prosperity in and of itself is not evil any more than money is—it is the attitude of our hearts and what we do with our prosperity that matter. If we prosper and it only makes us more greedy and selfish, then, yes, prosperity will not be a blessing for us; but, if we use our prosperity to secure the future of our families and to help others, then it will be a tool in our hands for good.

How many times do we see a need in the life of a son or daughter, or relative, or perhaps a friend or coworker, and wish that we could help meet that need? All around us there are people who need help to have food and the basic necessities of life. If we have a storehouse, we are in position to offer assistance to those in need. Without a storehouse, we miss opportunities to bless others.

Do We Want to Help Others?
Or Have Others Take Care of Us?

Like the grasshopper, if we do not have a storehouse, we are subconsciously planning for somebody else to take care of us. When we do not have a storehouse, we are constantly focused on our own needs rather than on the needs of others. Look again at Proverbs 6:7: the ant "having no captain, overseer or ruler, provides her supplies in the summer, and gathers her food in the harvest."

What would your life have been like if someone had personally taught you about finances during your youth? What if you had learned about the Storehouse Principle many years ago? Chances are that you, like most people, realize that you would be much better off today if you had learned these lessons long ago. But it's not too late to learn them. Look at the ant—the ant doesn't have a personal mentor. Nobody has to tell the ant to get busy, to produce, or to store up for the future. Nobody forces her to gather today and store for tomorrow. The ant doesn't look for help from anyone else to get ahead. The ant is a victor, not a victim. Ants work together as a community, helping each other. They don't wander around looking for other ants to support them. If we're not careful, we can cripple ourselves by making it a habit to rely on other people, or the government, to solve our problems for us.

Now, please don't misunderstand what is being said here. No man or woman is an island. God did not create us to be completely independent of other people. At times, we all need counseling. At times, we all need help. We need mentoring. We depend on other people for all kinds of things. Ants work in a community helping each other—we should do the same and realize that sometimes the burdens we face can take several of us to handle. But, if we're not careful, we can make ourselves so dependent on others that we expect them to be responsible for us instead of taking responsibility for ourselves. The welfare system in the United States was reformed several years ago because it was not helping people to help themselves. Instead, it encouraged too many people to become dependent on the welfare system itself, instead of accepting responsibility for their own lives. "Hand-outs" didn't really help people over the long term. What they needed were "hand-ups" that met pressing needs but also encouraged them to become providers rather than simply consumers. The ant accepts responsibility for meeting her own needs. The Bible says she is busy gathering and storing up food so that she can take care of herself.

Have you ever caught yourself daydreaming about someone paying all your bills and doing all your work? "Take care of me, honey." "Take care of me, government." "Take care of me, welfare." "Take care of me, Social Security." "Take care of me, boss." "Take care of me, company." "Take care of me, take care of me, take care of me." With that kind of thinking, we'll slide into a mindset of irresponsibility.

The Bible does not say that somebody is going to ride into our life like a knight on a white horse and rescue us from our financial problems. We can't expect anybody else to just walk up to us and hand us a million dollars!

We shouldn't expect anybody to make our mortgage payments for us. We shouldn't expect anybody to make our car payments for us. It's not right to believe that another human being is obligated to get us out of debt. Yet, many of us live our lives hoping that someone else will take care of us, or believing an inheritance from parents will someday, miraculously, "make us rich."

You Will Never Get Ahead Waiting for Someone Else

Consider the ant. She waits for no one. The ant just gets up in the morning and stretches her six legs and hits the road. She says by her actions, "I am not a victim. Life may throw some curves at me, but I'm bigger than the curves of life. Life has given me obstacles, but I will go around them. I will go over them. I will go through them, if necessary. I'm going to get there, bless God. I'm going to make it. I am not going to sit here waiting for someone else to solve my problems. I am going to do whatever I can today—even if it is only a little."

Some of us may have lost everything. We may not have a dime to our name. Perhaps we have filed bankruptcy or filed for welfare. Perhaps your home burned to the ground or you lost your job. Well, don't be a victim—go look at the ant. That may be where we are living today, but that's not where we will be tomorrow.

Proverbs 6:3 says, "Do this now my son and deliver thyself." Verse 5 says, "Deliver thyself as a roe from the hand of the hunter and as a bird from the hand of the fowler."

Your Future Begins Today

Wherever you are, your situation is not hopeless. Wherever you are today or whatever has happened to you in the past, start preparing for tomorrow. Look at what you have—whether it is time, talent, or treasure or any combination of these—and start building storehouses for your future. Build a spiritual storehouse, a natural storehouse, and a mental storehouse. Build storehouses for yourself, for your children, and for others. Determine to have reserves in every area of your life, so that whatever tries to knock you down will never knock you out.

If an ant can do it, surely God's children can do it as well. If a tiny insect can have determination, we can have determination. If a miniscule insect can be brave, we can be brave. And if the ant can be strong, we can be strong. If the ant can be wise enough to have a storehouse, then we should consider her ways and be just as wise! If we do, then who knows what great things God may do in our futures! The problem is that many of us are afraid to start. You may want to put it off a month or so before you begin. You may think something like, "Well, I can start saving something as soon as we pay off _____ (you fill in the blank)." But you cannot start from any place except where you are today. If Jesus is truly your Lord, than you need to obey Him in giving *and in saving*—and you need to start today! It is not enough to just be willing, or to just obey—you must do both! It is only those that are willing *and* obedient who will eat the best of the land.[1] And you have to be willing and obedient with what you have *now*, not what you only hope to have someday.

That is what happened to Van Crouch. When he heard this message from me in 1999, he became willing and obedient and put it into action—and he was blessed. But I'll let him tell you his story for himself.

---

[1] See Isaiah 1:19.

PART TWO

VAN'S STORY:

TAPPING INTO THE

STOREHOUSE MENTALITY

8

FROM THE OUTHOUSE
TO THE STOREHOUSE

**"What is more pleasing to the LORD: your burnt
offerings and sacrifices or your obedience to his voice?
Obedience is far better than sacrifice. Listening to him is
much better than offering the fat of rams."**

1 SAMUEL 15:22 NLT

Do you sometimes feel caught in a dog-eat-dog world wearing
Milk-Bone underwear?

That pretty much summed it up for me, when I first met Al Jandl
in 1987. With both of us being businessmen and ministers, we had
a good deal in common and a great deal of mutual respect so that
over the years we have developed a friendship. However, it wasn't
until 1999 that Al shared with me the principle that has revolution-
ized both my ministry and corporate speaking outreach in the years
since then. The financial peace it created for my wife and me has
been a key element to our stability and growth.

Our conversation took place after I had just spoken at his church
one weekend. We were standing near the lake in front of the guest
lodge for Victory Camp—which is where I usually stay when I speak

at Living Stones Church because the rooms in the lodge are nicer than those in some of the hotels in the area. As he handed me a check for my honorarium, and one to cover my expenses for the trip, he asked me a question that I had always expected someone to ask. What I didn't know, however, was that the answer I had so carefully prepared for that question over the years *was the wrong answer*.

The Big Question

"Van, I know you travel a great deal as a motivational speaker and minister. When you get a check like this, what do you do with it? How do you manage your money when it comes to you?"

"Al," I responded almost automatically, "I have always thought someone would ask me that question. I want you to know that we tithe off of the top of every check that comes in. Whenever we get a check, we take ten percent off the top and send it to other ministries we are partners with,"—at this point I named about six ministries that we give to regularly—"I do that with our ministry, our business, and our personal accounts. I want you to know that, beyond that, we are givers. All in all, we probably give around eighteen percent of our gross income. We are faithful givers to our partners."

An Even Bigger Question

He looked at me for a moment, considering what I had said. I expected him to be impressed with my answer, but the expression on his face didn't reflect the glowing approval I had envisioned. Finally, he said, "That is very commendable." Then he paused again. "But let me ask you this: Of all these ministries you give to, where are you on the list?"

"What?" I replied. This was not a question I had ever expected to be asked. "What do you mean?"

So he repeated the question, "Of all these ministries you give to, where is Van Crouch Communications on the list?"

"Um, it's not on the list."

"Don't you believe in what you do? Aren't you a ministry?"

"Well, yes, we are a ministry, and I believe in what I'm doing."

"Then why aren't you on the list? Don't you believe in what you are doing enough to give to it?"

I didn't know what to say. I stared at him somewhat blankly. What was he talking about? Giving to our own ministry? Wouldn't that be selfish?

"Let me ask you this way," he said when he saw that I had no response. "Do you want your ministry, your business, and your personal finances to be blessed?"

"Well, yes, of course!"

He paused again. "Well, why should God bless something that you don't believe in? Van, if I want to send money to any of those other ministries you just mentioned, why do I need you? I could write a check to them myself. When I write a check to Van Crouch Communications, then I am writing a check to Van Crouch

Communications, not a charitable organization that funnels my money to other ministries. Now if you want to give to those ministries, there is nothing wrong with that—it is even commendable—but do you give into your ministry? Do you have a storehouse for your ministry where you lay away some of every check that comes in so that you can be blessed?"

I am sure the confused look on my face was still there. "What do you mean?"

"Let me explain it to you this way: have you ever read Deuteronomy 28:8? It says, 'The LORD shall command the blessing upon thee in thy storehouses, and in all that thou settest thine hand unto; and he shall bless thee in the land which the LORD thy God giveth thee.' Van, God said He was going to bless your storehouse. Are you saying you don't have one?"

"No, I don't have any storehouse—I didn't know I was supposed to have a storehouse."

"Then let me ask you another question, 'How can God bless what you do not have?'"

"What's a Storehouse?"

"I don't know. What do you mean by a storehouse? Do you have a storehouse?"

"Van, you wouldn't believe the storehouses we have. I know that for a fact, because I can't believe them myself—I mean, I really have no idea how they got so large. All I do know is that, some twenty years back, we stumbled across a biblical principle and it revolution-ized our lives. We have never been so blessed. When we started a storehouse it was as if that was the key to opening heaven over us. Since then, we have never been in debt. We have paid cash for every-thing in our own lives and ministry: all the property you see here, all the buildings—even the church building and everything in it."

Then he paused again as an understanding of what he had just said dawned on my face. "Van, will you come to my office with me a minute? There is something else I want to do."

Now I was truly intrigued. "I would be glad to," I said.

As we walked across the camp and church campus towards his office, he continued, "Van, I am not bragging when I say that every-thing here is paid for. We don't owe on any of it and we paid cash for all of it. I don't like credit and I don't like paying interest for things that don't make me money. I have always been that way, maybe because I grew up so poor. I was poor all of my life until God showed me the principle from Deuteronomy 28:8 that He would command a blessing on my storehouses. I thought, 'If God is going to command a blessing on my storehouses, then I had better have one!' So I started one, and that was the beginning of all of this."

We walked the rest of the way in silence, but my mind was rac-ing. I looked around at everything there in a new light. *He doesn't owe anything on any of this? He owns hundreds of acres here! And he bought and paid for all of it with cash?*

Eventually we made our way across the street and entered the church building. We walked through the gorgeous entry area that was large enough to use for church banquets, through the bookstore, and back to his office—all of which were beautiful and well maintained. When we entered his office, I excused myself to go to the bathroom. Al picked up his telephone and had a short conversation with his administrative assistant. When I got back, Al had a check in his hand.

A New Start

Al looked at the check for a minute thinking again about what he was going to say. "Van, I want to give you another check. I want to teach you something. Now, please, don't take this check home with you to Chicago unless you promise that you will use it to start a savings account—a storehouse—for your ministry."

Now we had a savings account for our ministry, but there was nothing in it. Suddenly, I saw why. What Al was sharing with me was something I had never seen in the Bible before. Yet, as he said it, and as I looked around and saw what he had done by obeying the principle he was sharing with me, I knew what he was saying was true. I began to get excited about it. Suddenly, I saw that God wanted to take care of my family and me, not just all of the ministries with which we were partners.

So I determined at that moment that I would start calling our savings account a "storehouse" and that any money we put into it would stay there as a foundation for our ministry and not to pay our bills. I also determined that some of every check that came through our hands after that would go into that account—we wouldn't eliminate any partners, we would just add ourselves to the list. "Pastor Jandl," I said to him, "I will."

To be quite honest with you, I never expected what would come of that one simple act of obedience.

9

WATCH HOPE ARISE

Do two people walk hand in hand
if they aren't going to the same place?

Despite my promise to Pastor Jandl, I had one more hurdle to cross before I could open my storehouse account. I had to get the person who manages our business and personal accounts to understand what Pastor Al had taught me about the storehouse and get her to agree to start a storehouse fund and not use the money to pay bills. That person was my wife, Doni.

Our savings, in general, had always been a point of contention in our home, as it is in many marriages. In the eleven years that we had been married at that point, I cannot remember a time when we were not having financial difficulties of some type or another. Up until we established our storehouse, trying to get money to keep our ministry and home life running normally consumed much of my time and thought life. Many Christians will say, "Oh, I don't need a lot of money. God doesn't want us to be rich! God even said that it would be hard for the rich to enter heaven." But then they go out and spend sixty hours or more a week working to get money, and a good part of the rest of their time thinking about how to spend it or trying to figure out where it went! Another good part of the time, when they should be sleeping soundly, they toss and turn worrying about how they will ever be able to afford to put new tires on the car, send their kids to college or handle the most recent financial emergency—when they don't even have any savings! Then, there is the question of whether they will ever be able to retire! For people who don't want money, they sure spend a lot of time thinking about it!

What would be the trade-off if I could show you a way to spend that time thinking about God, playing with your kids, talking with your spouse, working in your church or community, or being a general blessing to others rather than worrying about the month that is still left to live after your paycheck has already run out?

It's Not About Making More Money— It's About Keeping It from Disappearing!

Much of the time, our financial crises were my fault. While I often focused on maximizing returns, Doni focused on rapid debt reduction and reducing the finance charges we were paying on everything. Not too long before this I had lost $8,000 in a "great investment" that in the end was more of a gamble than an investment. With my track record, I wasn't sure how Doni was going to react to my idea of a new investment plan called "our storehouse."

When I explained it to her, though, and showed her the scriptures it was based upon, she agreed to give it a try. We opened a separate savings account with the check that Pastor Jandl had given us, and then added a percentage from the honorarium check. Then, as regularly as we paid all of our other partnership pledges, we put a percentage into our storehouse each time we received a payment into our ministry, business, or personal lives. In fact, we started storehouses for all three. We were so literal about it that one time a temporary accountant who came in to work for us actually started looking around for our "storehouse" to put the check into as if it were a broom closet in our offices or something!

Inch by Inch, It's a Cinch!

It was amazing to me how that account suddenly started to grow—but in addition to that growth, other amazing things started happening. Where it had been difficult to pay our monthly bills before we had any storehouses, suddenly paying the electric and gas bills was easy. It didn't really make sense to us, either. It wasn't that we had a great deal of new income. In fact, because we were now saving a percentage, we should have had less, but somehow we always had the money in our general accounts to pay our bills when they came due. We started to operate in the storehouse blessings right from the beginning. I also discovered that by coming into agreement with my wife as to how we were going to operate the Storehouse Principle in our lives, we had also started to operate in another *commanded* blessing of the Bible.

The Bible's Other Commanded Blessing

As I have searched the scriptures, I have also noted that there are only three places that the Bible tells us that God will *command* a blessing, and two of them are directly on storehouses. Now think of this for a moment. The Bible is full of promises of blessings for those who follow God with all of their hearts, minds, souls, and bodies, but none of these promises says that God Himself will *command* the blessing. It is as if a system of blessings has been put into action in the same way that the planets were set into motion around the sun—God doesn't have to get involved further to give them an extra little push every now and then to keep them going. Yet, in these three passages, God gets personally involved and *commands* the blessing upon the people who operate in them.

The first of these is, of course, in the verse we have already looked at a couple of times:

> "The LORD will command the blessing on you in your
> storehouses and in all to which you set your hand,
> and He will bless you in the land which the LORD
> your God is giving you."
>
> DEUTERONOMY 28:8 NKJV

The second is actually found earlier in the Bible, but is also upon storehouses:

> Then I will command My blessing on you
> in the sixth year, and it will bring forth
> produce enough for three years.

> And you shall sow in the eighth year, and eat old produce
> until the ninth year; until its produce comes in, you shall
> eat of the old harvest.

LEVITICUS 25:21-22 NKJV

This commanded blessing was upon the crops that were to be stored while the land rested for the seventh year according to the economic system God set forth in the books of Moses. At the end of the sixth year, their harvest would be three times greater, because the people needed to be able to survive until the next planting season, rest the land for a year, and then have enough not only to plant the following year, but also to survive until those crops were harvested. All of these had to be put away in storehouses until they were needed.

The third commanded blessing was to be upon those who lived in unity or agreement:

> Behold, how good and how pleasant it is
> For brethren to dwell together in unity! . . .
>
> For there the LORD commanded the blessing—
> Life forevermore.

PSALM 133:1, 3 NKJV

I think this last reference holds a further key to the blessing of having a storehouse: that those who direct their storehouse must be in unity about how it is managed. If it is a family, there must be agreement between the husband and wife about how much is put into the storehouse from each check and when that money is to be taken out again.

The same agreement should exist between the leaders of a church that has a storehouse or the owners of a business who operate their finances according to the Storehouse Principle. This unity acts as a safeguard to keep the storehouse from being abused— money should only be taken out of it if all those responsible for it agree that they are directed by God to do so, and even then it should only be done on extremely rare occasions. This added blessing of agreement is one that should add increased peace to our daily lives:

> **"Again I say to you that if two of you agree on earth concerning anything that they ask, it will be done for them by My Father in heaven.**
>
> **"For where two or three are gathered together in My name, I am there in the midst of them."**
>
> **MATTHEW 18:19-20** NKJV

Yet Another Storehouse Blessing

In addition to having enough to regularly pay all of our bills, something else began to happen. Suddenly, my work was not the grind that it used to be. Don't misunderstand, I love what I do and get to meet a lot of great people through my speaking engagements, both in churches of excellence around the country as well as in businesses and community groups, but there was always something missing when I would arrive home, hand the check to our accountant, *and know that it was already spent.* The money I had just earned was already gone, so I was already playing catch-up again. It was a constant race to just keep up. I had money to give all the time because we had determined to tithe off of the top whenever money came in, but I will be quite honest with you, I am not too sure I was a cheerful giver.[1] I don't think I ever realized this, though, until the stability of having a storehouse began to set in.

After just a few months of having the storehouse, I began to realize that when I handed a check to our accountant, the bills were already paid and some of the check I was handing over would go into our reserves. I knew that if I didn't speak the next weekend, that we would be okay and we could survive. This didn't mean that I worked any less, but suddenly work was *less like work*, if you know what I mean. It was no longer a *have to* but a *want to*. It was no longer a struggle to keep up, but the security of getting another step ahead. In just a few short years, I suddenly built more financial peace into our lives than I had in all the time of working before that. It was an amazing confidence builder.

Again, don't misunderstand; it wasn't as if we had never saved money before. I have a 403b retirement plan I have always given to faithfully, and we had always tried to save, but it had never worked like this before. Having a storehouse was much more than just saving. It was obeying God and activating His wisdom in all that we did. Suddenly, we had a hope and a future as we had never had before!

---

[1] See 2 Corinthians 9:7.

An Added Blessing of Financial Peace

I also noticed that a good deal of tension in my marriage disappeared. Without the constant financial pressure, Doni and I were more in agreement in all that we did. I felt as if she saw me as a new person—no longer was I the guy who always lost or spent our money, but now I was the guy who had introduced the principle that was securing our financial future. Every check we wrote to our storehouses was another brick on the firm foundation of God's Word to solidify our home against any storm that could attack us. Little did we know when we started that the stability of that home would help see us through a storm that threatened to cost Doni her life.

It was only a few years after starting our storehouse that we discovered that Doni had stage-four liver cancer. It is very hard to describe what that type of news can do to a person. As a minister, I pray for a lot of people who need healing when I travel, but when disease hits your own home, it is very different. It shakes your faith to its very foundations, and you have to believe for healing every day regardless of the circumstances facing you. We suddenly, and unexpectedly, entered a fight for Doni's life.

So, for the next full year or so, we fought the cancer through medicine and prayer. It was good to know that, in the midst of the treatments, our financial situation was no longer a major source of pressure for us. If I needed to cancel my meetings for a few weeks to spend time with Doni as she recovered from her treatments, then

I could. It's not that she was healed just because we had a storehouse, but in the midst of such trying times, it was a tremendous blessing not to have the added pressures of having to worry about paying our bills in addition to fighting the cancer.

All the while, we stayed faithful to putting money into our storehouse and God continued to bless us. We accumulated medical bills during this time that could have easily wiped out all of our storehouse, yet God gave us favor with our insurance company, and we never had to touch our savings to cover the expenses. We fought a fight of faith daily all that time, believing that God would give wisdom to the doctors to do exactly what was needed to help heal Doni and that God would add His healing power to their treatments. What we saw was that her survival depended on doing everything that we could to keep our attitudes positive, so we listened to uplifting praise and worship tapes and CDs—and of course, took in mega-doses of the Word of God. We had to take every thought captive and let nothing negative into our thinking. It is hard to say what would have happened had we also had the added pressures of financial problems to face as we were going through this time, but it was definitely a blessing that we didn't.

Despite the physical attack, in January of 2003 Doni received a clean bill of health from the doctors. The cancer was completely gone. To us, the financial blessing of the storehouse is only the very tip of the iceberg of the Storehouse Principle blessings. What obedience to God in this principle has done to restore hope and peace in my family is unfathomable. I have seen it happen so often with others now that I know God will do the same thing for you if you are willing to put the Storehouse Principle into action in your life.

10

A NEW WAY OF THINKING

"Whoever can be trusted with very little can also be trusted
with much, and whoever is dishonest with very little
will also be dishonest with much. So if you have not been
trustworthy in handling worldly wealth,
who will trust you with true riches? And if you have not been
trustworthy with someone else's property,
who will give you property of your own?

"No servant can serve two masters. Either he will hate the
one and love the other, or he will be devoted to the one and
despise the other. You cannot serve both God and Money."

LUKE 16: 10-13 NIV

One of my first steps in trying to get a better understanding of the
Storehouse Principle after Pastor Jandl shared it with me was to go
to the Bible and see what it said about money. From knowing him for
as long as I had, I believed there was more to his storehouse blessing
than just putting money in the bank. Somehow, he had latched onto
a spiritual truth upon which he had built a level of financial peace
that seemed to defy explanation. I knew that the Storehouse
Principle was the foundation for this peace, but that there were also

other attitudes and wisdom operating in his life concerning how he dealt with money that took that blessing even further.

The storehouse principle had created a different mentality in him than any I had experienced in other ministers who had also been financially successful. It was a mentality I wanted to tap into. Some say that things like that are more caught then taught, which I believe is true to a large degree; but I also knew that if it was something that we needed in our lives, then it would be found in God's Word.

What I have found in that search has amazed me. It has transformed how I view money. It revealed several misconceptions that I had held about what money really is and why I had always had such a problem in dealing with it. I also found that there were some traditions I had held about wealth that were on such a subconscious level that I had never even realized how they were hindering me. It is often only through the mirror of the Bible that we can separate those things that are truly spiritual from those things that are merely intellectual and come to a truth that will set us free from bondage.

Is Money Evil?

Historically, money and Christianity have seemed at odds since the disciples first asked Jesus, "Who then can be saved?" in response to His statement, "It is easier for a camel to get through the eye of a needle than for a rich man to get into the kingdom of God."[1] The church has time and time again been derailed from its mission to

---

[1] See Matthew 19:24 and Mark 10:25.

spread the Gospel of Jesus Christ as it has been corrupted by the deceitfulness of riches, the cares of this world, and the lust for other things. As happens too often, prosperity can lead to complacency, and complacency can lead to a loss of purpose and focus in life. Because of this, wealth has come to be viewed by many as the opposite of Christian charity and spirituality. "Too much money" has been seen as something like "too much temptation": the more of it we have, the more likely we are to fall into sin that will destroy our lives, if not our eternal futures.

When we set sail to get a proper biblical understanding of what God really thinks about money, then we also travel the murky waters of selfish desires and hidden agendas—just below the surface are issues within our hearts that we would rather not bring to light. We are often unaware of these attitudes, as I realized I was. Issues of self-esteem, covetousness, self-image, and self-discipline all affect what we think about and how we handle money. Often, we come to some of the toughest crossroads in our lives when we realize that we have adopted certain teachings, without even thinking about them, more to appease our self-concept and personal desires than out of a pursuit to live the truth. We make small compromises that eventually lead us to accept half-truths that entrap us. When we bring these to light, however, God can bring us back to the true blessings He wants so much for us to live in.

To live in this freedom, there are a few basic things that we should first understand about the nature of money. If we grasp these concepts, it is much easier to build the financial stability, freedom, and wealth that will make us more effective in our God-given dreams and purposes rather than lapse into the "trust in riches" that can be our downfall.

#1. Money Can Be a Force.

Most of us see money as an inanimate object; we confuse the bills in our wallet with the conceptual entity that money truly is. *Money*, however, is not the gold, diamonds, gems, or paper certificates that we use to represent it and barter with. *Money* is the concept of faith behind those things that ascribes value to them. As such, money is almost alive. Like electricity or water, it is in constant flux and movement and is rarely stagnant. When it flows, it moves other things along with it. It creates power to make things happen. Whether that movement is creative or destructive is greatly determined by the way it is handled.

Let me give you some examples. Water flowing in a river can move a waterwheel to grind grain or generate electricity, or it can flood around a house and tear it from its foundations. It can wear away at a cliff until the side of the hill crumbles. Electricity can flow through a wire to create light or strike a tree in the form of lightning to blow it apart or start a forest fire.

Money works in much the same way. It can be used to build a skyscraper, a hospital, a church, or a home, or it can turn people to greed and selfishness that will undermine the stability of a family or nation.

This nature is reflected in the fact that when Jesus talks about wealth, He personifies it. This is perhaps best seen in the *King James Version* of the Bible where the translators tried to catch this by calling it Mammon:

> **No man can serve two masters: for either**
> **he will hate the one, and love the other; or else**
> **he will hold to the one, and despise the other.**
> **Ye cannot serve God and mammon.**

MATTHEW 6:24

This word only appears four places in the scriptures, here and three times in Luke 16. If you look in Bible references such as *Strong's Concordance* and *Vine's Expository Dictionary*, you will see that it not only means "wealth," but also personifies it—it becomes an idol, like the stone representation of an ancient pagan god. It could also be called "greed", "covetousness", or even more simply "selfishness". The more we "love money," after all, the more *selfish* we are.

It is interesting to note that Jesus never told us we have a choice to serve either God or the devil—he said we have a choice to serve either God or *wealth*. We have a choice to either follow the Living Creator or make an idol out of the natural concept of money.

Money is a tool, or resource, that can help us do things—nothing more, nothing less. It motivates people, and enough of it can move mountains. It is not a God, to be sought after with our whole hearts, nor an end in itself. This is why trusting in riches is foolishness. The man who trusts in his hammer more than in the designer of a house is a fool, but he is not a fool for using a hammer or two to follow the designer's plans.

#2. In Itself, Money Has No Character or Morality.

How many times have we heard the misquotation "Money is the root of all evil"? Usually, however, someone will catch the error and correct it: "You know it isn't 'money that is the root of all evil', but *the love of* money that is the root of all evil.' God doesn't care if we have money as much as He cares if money has us."

Money, in itself, is not good or evil, although, as we have already discussed, it can be used as a tool to do good or evil. As St. Ambrose said, "Just as riches are an impediment to virtue in the wicked, so in the good they are an aid of virtue." If it becomes an idol in our lives—if we "love it" more than God—then it will magnify the destruction and "evil" within us. Money as "lord" is an exacting taskmaster working all kinds of evil from the smallest hurts to the largest cruelties.

#3. Money Reveals the Integrity
   ## and Stability of Any Person or System.

Send 120 watts through an ordinary light bulb for your home, and you will get a warm glow that you can read by. Send a billion watts suddenly through that same bulb and you are liable to have an explosion. Attach a garden hose to the faucet outside of your home and you can easily wash your car or water your lawn. Attach that same hose to a fire hydrant and it will burst and be useless, and the water will flow everywhere.

A faulty electrical system can often handle low voltage without a problem, but pump up the power, and if there is a weakness, you will find it pretty quickly—and, hopefully, before it catches anything on fire.

Money, like pressure on the outside of a tube of toothpaste, reveals what is inside. People are not greedy because they have money. They were always greedy; you just never saw the greed until they had enough money to do something about it. Notice that Paul didn't say, "The love of money that rich people have is the root of all evil," but just that "the love of money is the root of all evil" and that those who seek after it "fall into a temptation and a snare." A poor person that mugs and robs a man does not do it because of his wealth, but because they loved money more than doing what is right. Getting money becomes the only goal—and the means to getting it become corrupt.

A greedy, hateful person with no resources can't do much, but put him at the head of a government with its armies and finances to command and he may soon be on the road to destruction. If Hitler had been kept in jail and had never become the head of the German state, would World War II ever have happened?

People don't have these things in their hearts because money put them there. Greed, selfishness, and covetousness are locked up in our sin nature—it is just that we don't really see much of it come out until that person has enough money to do some real damage.

We don't have to have money to love money! What is the sin of the twenty-first century that is the root of all evil? The sin of wanting what others have or being eager to acquire more—in other words, the simple drive to "keep up with the Joneses" or envy. If this is the driving force behind most of what you do in your life, then you serve money, not God. From it, all other forms of evil emerge.

Just as money can't buy you happiness, the lack of it can't keep people from being miserable either. Money is not a deciding factor as to whether or not people are selfish and covetous, it only reveals the true nature of the people it comes to or the systems it runs through.

#4. Work Must Be Done to Make Money a Positive, Creative Force.

Pouring water down your chimney would do more harm than good, but put that same water through a system of pipes and faucets and it has any number of uses. Run it through a turbine and it will create power. It must be directed to do good. In a home, pipes and faucets have to be built and carefully maintained—and they don't just appear out of thin air or last forever without repairs from time to time.

Money is the same way. If we have a system for managing it, it will have tremendous blessing for our families, but if we just let it flow freely, without any direction, we are working towards a disaster. If we have a money management system that has weaknesses in it, more money will only increase the problems caused by those weaknesses and make them more difficult to fix. Problems of that nature are more easily fixed when the pressure is smaller (less money is flowing through) than when things are already out of control. As the Bible says, those who are faithful in little will be faithful in much, and those unfaithful in little will only increase their unfaithfulness if they get more. Whether we have a little or a lot, the key is to be faithful with it.

#5. The Best Way to Keep Money from Mastering You Is to Master It.

If you don't have a good system for handling the electricity that flows through your home, you will be constantly at work fixing it. It will take up all of your time and more than its fair share of your thought life and devotion. You will be constantly replacing bulbs, appliances, switching breakers, and, perhaps quite literally, putting out fires.

Money is the same way. If you don't control your cash flow—how money flows through your home—then it will determine what you do with your free time, what schools your children will attend, whether you drive a lemon or a nice safe car to take your family around in, how much of your time, talents, and treasures you give to the Gospel, how you will speak to your spouse, when you will retire, or whether or not you can retire—in effect, it will dictate almost everything you will do in your entire life. If you control money, however, then these decisions will remain in your hands.

You Have to Take Control

Certainly, wealth has taken a lot of the blame for the problems we face in our world today, but that is like blaming the water because your basement flooded. The problem is not the water; it's your rusted and corrupted pipes! Our world has problems because people's hearts are rusted and corrupted with greed and selfishness. If we are going to get control of how money flows through our lives—as a blessing or as a curse—then we need to first "fix" these heart issues.

An interesting thing that I discovered as we started to operate in the Storehouse Principle, however, has been that as we began to build up a "reservoir" in our home in case the "water" should ever stop flowing in, it made us begin to take inventory of these issues in our hearts and analyze our financial management systems to fix the leaks on our own. We began to tell our money what to do rather than allowing it to dictate to us the course of our lives. We suddenly found that operating correctly in this natural area was also a great way to exercise our spiritual fruit and help it grow. By exercising patience, wisdom, and self-control in dealing with money, the spiritual fruit began to also pour into other areas. By letting God be Lord of our finances, He used them to teach us to be better servants to Him in all areas of our lives.

By taking hold of our financial problems, God has helped us to deal with spiritual problems that would have otherwise gone unaddressed. And learning to be faithful with "unrighteous mammon" has become a way for God to produce true riches in our lives. If you will start to repair your financial house by using this principle, God will open you up to more true, spiritual riches as well!

11

GETTING TO THE ROOT
OF THE PROBLEM

**They that will be rich fall into temptation and a snare,
and into many foolish and hurtful lusts,
which drown men in destruction and perdition.**

**For the love of money is the root of all evil:
which while some coveted after, they have erred
from the faith, and pierced themselves through
with many sorrows.**

1 TIMOTHY 6:9-10

The original Greek word translated as "the love of money" in 1 Timothy 6:10 is the word *philarguria*, which is a combination of the words *phileo*, "to love," and *arguros*, "silver." So, literally, this word means "the love of silver" or "the love of money." First Timothy 6:10 is the only place in the Bible where this word appears in this form. When we look at this word translated in this way, most of us might feel pretty safe from its clutches. "I don't 'love money,'" we reason, "I don't even have any! Jesus said that it was hard for rich people to enter into heaven! Ha! No worries there! I am anything but rich!"

However, if you look at your *Strong's Concordance,* you will see that this word comes from the Greek word *philarguros*, which appears twice in the Bible, once earlier in 1 Timothy:

> **This know also, that in the last days perilous times shall come. For men shall be lovers of their own selves, *covetous*, boasters, proud, blasphemers, disobedient to parents, unthankful, unholy, without natural affection, trucebreakers, false accusers, incontinent, fierce, despisers of those that are good, traitors, heady, high-minded, lovers of pleasures more than lovers of God; having a form of godliness, but denying the power thereof: from such turn away.**
>
> 1 TIMOTHY 3:1-5 *[italics added]*

and just after the passage quoted at the beginning of the last chapter from Luke 16:

> **The Pharisees, *who loved money* [were *covetous* (KJV)], heard all this and were sneering at Jesus.**
>
> LUKE 16:14 NIV *[italics and insert added]*

They didn't like what Jesus was telling them about money, because He was showing them the nature of their own hearts by what he was teaching. They were covetous—in other words, *they loved money*—therefore they did not serve God as they professed that they did, but served their own selfish desires instead—they served money.

According to *The American Heritage Dictionary of the English Language*, the word *covetous* means "excessively . . . desirous; . . . greedy. . . . eager for acquisition." So Paul's earlier advice about money might also be put this way: "Greed, desire of what others have, or the excessive eagerness to acquire more material wealth is the root of all evil." A simpler translation of this same Greek word would be "selfishness." If you are striving in any way to get more material wealth, you are in danger of being a lover of money!

Beware of "Stuffitis"!

Before I go any further though, let me clarify this thought so that there is no confusion. Blatant materialism involves acquiring stuff to make yourself feel better about yourself. Author and radio host Dave Ramsey, however, says that most of us are not materialistic—what we have is called *stuffitis*. Stuffitis is the insatiable desire to have the best stuff. We don't just want a car; we want a Mercedes or BMW convertible, or the biggest SUV or pickup available. We don't just want a refrigerator that keeps things cold, we want one that speaks to us, dispenses cold drinks, and makes sandwiches for halftime. But having the nicest stuff is often a relative thing—relative to what our friends and neighbors have, for example. In other words, it's the old desire to "keep up with the Joneses." We need to have a nicer car, bigger boat, or larger RV parked in our front yard than the neighbors do, otherwise we feel inferior. Stuffitis has driven many Americans to incredible financial difficulties though, as they have bought all of their nice stuff on credit! Then, when their bills come due, they wonder how they got into this fix!

Money Doesn't Buy Happiness

If acquiring material things becomes our sole ambition in life, it crowds out wisdom, and reveals that the love of money controls our lives. If we mortgage our futures—and our families' futures!—in order to fulfill our lust for "stuff" today, we can wreak financial havoc in our lives and in the lives of those around us.

Am I off my rocker? Then let me just mention a few current buzzwords: "Arthur Anderson," "Enron," "WorldCom/MCI"—or any of the other companies that have gone into financial ruin in recent years because their management teams were driven by the desire to line their own pockets. Think of the human suffering that has been caused by this! Some people take old-fashioned shortcuts to get ahead: lying, cheating and stealing. They mortgage the future in the name of immediate enjoyment, and the byproducts of greed are not pretty at all. In the end, it never pays to step on others while climbing the ladder of success. Conscience is a stubborn thing and some greedy souls try to "cope" with their guilt by turning to drugs, alcohol, pornography, or more immediate forms of suicide. Crime and corruption can happen in the pursuit of money and the lust for material things. In the name of greed, parents can spend long hours at the office while neglecting their families. Or, they may drive their children mercilessly to succeed so that they can "get into the best colleges" and "have better lives"—all in the pursuit of material wealth.

Getting to the Root of the Problem

No wonder the Bible tells us that all forms of evil emerge from this selfishness, this desire to get ahead at all cost, this greed, this "love of money." It erupts from the fear that doing things God's way is not enough to be happy—that we have to grab what we can on our own. If we do that, we replace God on the throne of our lives with money, and money is a cruel taskmaster that drives people to their brink—worry, stress, heart disease, marital failure, even crime. If we serve money, then we bow at the feet of the god of this world's system of lust and greed. If we exalt selfishness, we serve material wealth—we serve mammon instead of God.

This certainly happens in the business world. Yet, in the midst of the chaos, deception, corporate greed, and CEO mismanagement that exists today, there are many companies that operate with integrity, vision, character, and the financial stability of having storehouses. In fact, a major reason why these companies succeed is that they operate using godly principles. Their management teams would love to have plush offices and lavish salary packages, as some of their competitors do, but they won't sacrifice their financial stability or principles to get them.

In others words, "the love of money" is not all powerful. Many business leaders have chosen to be motivated by soundness, and not selfishness. Their companies are a blessing to their employees and to the communities around them, even as they prosper financially. They "do well" by "doing good." We ought to follow their example, as "storehouse people," and be a blessing to our families and others around us.

Getting More Money May Not Be the Answer to Your Problems

If the love of money directs our lives, we're like the dog that keeps straining at the rope that has him tied to a tree. Whatever the dog wants always seems to be just beyond his reach. The dog keeps straining, and stretching the rope as far as it will go, but no matter how far he stretches it, what he wants remains just beyond his reach. He is not content to live with the things that have been provided for him—for some reason, he seems convinced that what will really make him happy is the stuff that's just beyond his reach. The grass seems greener wherever the rope won't allow him to go.

If you consider that the dog is like the average American, and that the rope is the average American's normal monthly income, then you get an unfortunate picture of how many Americans live—continually at the end of their means. Worse yet, if the rope represents the *credit limit* of the average American, than you have a picture of constant financial stress and imminent financial disaster! The problem is, no matter how long the rope is, the dog will always strain at the end of it for what lies beyond. The Apostle Paul might just as easily have said that the root of all evil is the "love of stuff" as the "love of money." Regardless of what you call it, this is the desire—basically selfishness—that is the root of all the bad things that happen in the world today. It wasn't enough for Adam and Eve to have the Garden of Eden, as beautiful and opulent as it was— they selfishly wanted more, and that desire for more lost them everything that they had.

More rope is not the answer for that dog any more than more money is the answer for most of us. The answer is being content with what is well within reach of the rope and always having extra "rope" left over. We have to be faithful in little before we can be faithful in much.[1] This is what having a storehouse does. When we add to our storehouse each time money comes into our hands (by spending less than we take in), the desire for what is currently beyond our reach lessens—it is put into its right place as a lesser priority. The Storehouse Principle keeps us focused on real needs rather than selfish desires and disciplines us to live well within our means—and that gives us the power to be content. It brings peace into our lives from Jesus Christ our Prince of Peace.

[1] See Luke 19:17.

12

HAS YOUR UPKEEP BECOME YOUR DOWNFALL?

Godliness with contentment is great gain.

1 TIMOTHY 6:6

I have often preached from the pulpit the old saying "If your outflow exceeds your income, then your upkeep will become your downfall." Despite my preaching, it was still happening to us—our upkeep was such a downfall for us that it was keeping me up nights. Yet, when we started regularly putting money into our storehouses, we saw this trend reverse. Little by little, we pulled ahead of the demands of our financial obligations.

I have noticed an amazing thing that happens when you tithe: the ninety percent you have left will go farther than the original one hundred percent. This is a blessing of God. If God can do this with ninety percent, why can't He also do it with eighty-five percent when you tithe and then put five percent in your storehouse? Or with eighty-seven percent as you give ten to God and three to your storehouse? The truth of the matter is that He can and does, if we are obedient in our giving *and* our savings. Remember, God doesn't specify how much you put into your storehouse each time, so I don't want to, either. The point is to start doing it. Even if you only put a dollar in out of each check that comes your way, you will begin to activate the principle. The main point is to get started; and once you do get started, be ready for God to teach you how to stretch your money.

If you obey God's Word in tithing, giving, *and* putting reserves away into your storehouse, God will give you the wisdom to make the remainder go farther than the original amount otherwise would have gone. He will do this by helping you correct your attitudes regarding money and by using self-control and patience to make your money work more effectively for you. As we obey His Word, we will also reap the blessings of obedience. We need to be open to be led by Him in every area of our lives—whether it is in the financial realm or any other area of our lives.

The Bible clearly tells us that we should not expect to be blessed if we live like worldly people who merely serve themselves. The power of God can keep us from sin, and God wants us to avoid the gross immorality of the world around us. But God wants us to do more than just avoid doing things that are bad. He also directs us to do things that are good—like manage money properly and build wealth to carry out His purposes. God wants us to live apart from this world's system, and according to His system, in all things, including the management of wealth. God desires that we escape the corruption that is in the world in order to enjoy His spiritual blessings of peace and holiness; and he also desires that we escape the financial bondage of the world's system (based on lust and greed) to enjoy His natural blessings of having our needs met, paying our bills on time, being a blessing to others, and being able to retire comfortably when the appropriate time comes.

We Need to Change Our Thinking

The culture in which we live trains us from the time we are young to live a lifestyle that will keep us enslaved to money our whole lives. God doesn't want us to be slaves to money; He wants money to be a tool for us so that we have the freedom to follow Him with our whole hearts.

From the time we are young, we are taught to want *things*: toys, games, clothes, etc., before we even understand the value of a dollar. We are bombarded with commercials as we watch cartoons on television, and whenever we visit someone else's house we are amazed at the room full of toys and games that they have that are so different from our own. We are taught to equate fun with what we have. More fun is always available around the corner if we just get that new thing as our next birthday or Christmas present. We are even taught to start planning our lists months in advance. We are taught to be discontented with what we have and to want new things on almost a continual basis.

This continues after we become adults. Our culture urges us to set goals more for what we want—a nice car, a new house, a country club or health spa membership—than for what we will do with our lives and who we will be. If we still don't understand the value of a dollar, we might go head-over-heels in debt to acquire the things that we want. Even if we do put some money away in savings, or build equity in our homes, we are bombarded with advice to borrow against those assets to buy that new car, go on vacation, or consolidate our credit card debt. After all, if you take out a second mortgage on your home, the interest payments are tax deductible! (Though, of course, you would have more money in your pocket if you weren't paying any interest at all!) This advice is aimed at keeping us in debt perpetually.

Consider these facts and statistics for a moment:

- Eighty percent of graduating college seniors have credit card debt before they even have jobs. Nearly one fifth of all people who filed for bankruptcy in 2002 were college students.

- Ninety percent of people in the U.S. buy things they don't have the cash to pay for. A recent study in the *Wall Street Journal* states that seven out of ten Americans live from paycheck to paycheck.

- Americans, on average, have a total of eleven credit obligations on record with credit bureaus. Of these, seven are likely to be credit cards.

- The average American has a combined limit of $12,000 on all of their credit cards. Almost fifteen percent of Americans are using eighty percent or more of their available credit card limits. The average American family carries a credit card balance of over $5,000.

- The average U.S. household carries $18,700 in debt, not including a home mortgage.

- Three fifths of all Americans don't pay off their credit card balances every month. Because of this, the average cost of something purchased with a credit card is 112 percent higher (more than twice as much!) than if they had paid cash for the same item.

- Nearly half of all Americans have reserves and savings equal to less than one month's expenses. If they lost their jobs, they would be in immediate trouble and probably live off of their credit cards exclusively until they either find a new job or go bankrupt.

- By age 65, most Americans who have worked all of their lives still can't write a check for $5,000!

- Near the end of the 1980s, the typical American family saved just under eight percent of its income. By the end of the 1990s, that same household spent a tenth of a percent *more* than it earned.

Saving or Spending?

When I was growing up, all of the schools had programs and posters everywhere about buying U.S. Savings Bonds. Today, our kids receive letters in the mail offering them credit cards! Today's world financial system is set up so that your money is gone before you ever earn it. This is one of the reasons why the Bible tells us not to love the things of the world[1]—God wants us to operate in a different cycle than this one of materialism and debt—He wants us to live in a cycle of blessing!

A first key to combating the cycle of debt and lack is to be *content* with what we have. As 1 Timothy 6 says:

> **Godliness actually is a means of great gain**
> **when accompanied by contentment.**
>
> **For we have brought nothing into the world,**
> **so we cannot take anything out of it either.**
>
> **If we have food and covering,**
> **with these we shall be content.**
>
> 1 TIMOTHY 6:6-8 NASB (*italics added*)

The word that is translated "contentment" in 1 Timothy 6:6 is the Greek word *autarkeia*, which, oddly enough, is only found in this form in one other place in the Bible, where it is translated "suf-

---

[1] See 1 John 2:15-16.

ficiency." This is when Paul is discussing taking up a special offering for the believers in Jerusalem:

> So I thought it necessary to urge the brethren that they would go on ahead to you and arrange beforehand your previously promised bountiful gift, so that the same would be ready as a bountiful gift and not affected by covetousness.
>
> Now this I say, he who sows sparingly will also reap sparingly, and he who sows bountifully will also reap bountifully.
>
> Each one must do just as he has purposed in his heart, not grudgingly or under compulsion, for God loves a cheerful giver.
>
> And God is able to make all grace abound to you, so that always having all *sufficiency* in everything, you may have an abundance for every good deed.

1 CORINTHIANS 9:5-8 NASB (*italics added*)

For years I have heard 1 Corinthians 9:8—"God is able to make all grace abound to you, so that always having all *sufficiency* in everything, you may have an abundance for every good deed"—true biblical prosperity. That if we would obey God in our giving, He would make all grace (including financial blessings) abound to us so that we would always have all we need to be a blessing in everything we do. However, when I saw that the word *sufficiency* in this passage could also be translated *contentment*, it gave it a whole different emphasis to my understanding of biblical prosperity. In other words, being content with what we have—saying literally that "It is enough," or "What I have now is sufficient to make me happy"—is a necessity to being *truly* rich. It is the act of "putting money in its place," if you will, letting it know that God is our Lord and earning money to pay our bills is not. It doesn't mean that we stop working or never buy new things or get presents for our children anymore, it just means that we do such things on a cash rather than credit basis and control our spending rather than letting it control us.

Be Content with What You Have

If we are willing to be content with what we have, God will show us how to stretch our money to get what we need or desire. We need to learn to save up money to buy things that are outside of our normal expenditures and not buy them on credit. Not only that, but if we exercise patience and prayer, God will also show us how to pay less to get the same things. He will teach us to be frugal so that we can do more with less.

If we are willing to save regularly, then we will have the assets available to purchase the things we want when the right deal comes along. Self-control, patience, and planning will replace impulse buying and worrying about finance charges. Financial peace will replace materialism. We will replace the time spent worrying over our bills with more important things—like being with family, helping at church, praying, or evangelizing our neighborhoods.

Will You Serve Money or God?

God didn't design us to serve money, but our "buy now" culture seems as if it would like nothing better than to see us all working sixty-to-ninety-hour weeks—at the office rather than at home or in church—and with no reserves, no retirement fund, no money put away for our children's education, and always only a half step ahead of our creditors. God has not called us to live like that. If we want to live differently than those who live according to the ungodly system of the world, then we have to do things differently than they do. We need to get out of the "buy it now on credit because I want it now" mentality and into the "save for the future and only pay cash" storehouse mentality.

13

POSITIONED TO MAKE A DIFFERENCE

Keep your lives free from the love of money and be content with what you have, because God has said,
"Never will I leave you;
never will I forsake you."

So we say with confidence,
"The Lord is my helper; I will not be afraid.
What can man do to me?"

HEBREWS 13:5-6 NIV

In their best-selling book, *The Millionaire Next Door: The Surprising Secrets of America's Wealth*, Tom Stanley and William Danko revealed a surprising thing about the majority of America's millionaires, something that we never would have guessed from what we usually see about the wealthy from television and magazines: that *they are frugal*. In their study of America's wealthy, they found that one of the main reasons these people were wealthy was because they valued financial security more than taking part in the rat race. They found that most millionaires live in solid, safe, middle class neighborhoods and invest their money in their children and their future rather than in their status. They want to be friends with the "Smiths" and avoid "keeping up with the Jones." They want to *live* a quality of life and not just *show* it, and they hate to waste money just for the privilege of "looking good to the neighbors."

Think about this for a moment: which would make you happier and give you more peace? Living the lifestyle that you have right now, but having a million dollars in the bank; or having a million dollars worth of stuff crammed into your house, and nothing in the bank? It's pretty obvious what the best answer is, isn't it? And that is the same decision that most of America's millionaires have made: they would rather have the money in the bank and the security it brings for themselves and their families.

Living within Your Means Brings Peace

A man who learned the Storehouse Principle from Al, named Tim Brooks[1] once told a story that illustrates this very well. Someone came to him with the opportunity to buy an expensive car for a fraction of its retail cost. Excited about the possibility of driving a fancy car, Tim started pursuing the deal until a friend of his warned him of what he was getting himself into.

"Tim," he told him, "Even if he gave you that car, you couldn't afford to keep it running. The windshield wiper blades for that car are $75 apiece and it costs $300 just to change the oil, much less

---

[1] Tim Brooks' inspiring testimony is in chapter sixteen of this book.

have any other work done on it. You don't need that car for your work and there is no other practical reason for you to have it other than impressing other people when they see you driving it. That car will cost you more in the long run than what you have now, and what you have now is pretty nice. Are you sure you want to put out all of that extra cash just to look better?"

In the end, Tim counted the cost and decided that he didn't need to have that car. Having such a prestigious car was not as valuable to him as saving money and putting it into his storehouse. As Jesus advised, he counted all of the costs before taking the next step:

> "For which of you, intending to build a tower,
> does not sit down first and count the cost, whether
> he has enough to finish it—lest, after he has laid
> the foundation, and is not able to finish,
> all who see it begin to mock him, saying, 'This man began
> to build and was not able to finish.'"

LUKE 14:28-30 NKJV

This Principle Will Work for Anyone

While the modern media covers rock stars, celebrities, and athletes who sign multi-million dollar contracts only to go bankrupt later in divorce settlements or career declines, contemporary books about real long-term millionaires show how modern-day millionaires have applied the Storehouse Principle to amass wealth, many times without even realizing it. According to Tom Stanley and William Danko's research, the average American millionaire looks something like this:

- About eighty percent of them are from the first generation of their families to be wealthy, and they do not see themselves at a disadvantage if they did not receive an inheritance.

- Only one in five does not hold at least a college degree, and many have advanced degrees beyond college. They believe education is very important and are more willing to spend money on it than on luxuries for their homes. They spend heavily on the education of their offspring.

- They don't necessarily have flashy jobs, but two-thirds of them do work for themselves. They may be welding contractors, auctioneers, pest controllers, or paving contractors.

- Most of them have only been married once, and most of the wives in these families do not work outside of their homes.

- They live well below their means, wear inexpensive clothing, and very few drive brand new cars. They live in nice, but not lavish, homes. To look at them, you would not know that on average they are worth more than $3.5 million.

- They have saved and/or invested fifteen to twenty percent of their earned income every year. For many of them, their main hobby is managing their investment funds.

- They are careful planners, budgeters, and investors.

- They have enough savings that they could continue to live for at least ten years without working. They have added to their savings funds throughout their lives without planning to spend this money.

- They built their wealth up gradually through their working years, and not in one fell swoop. Their average age is about 57 years old, but only one out of five of them is retired.

Don't Wait for Your Ship to Come In

These people operate their lives with a very different mentality than most. They didn't just wait for their ship to come in, and didn't buy lottery tickets hoping to strike it rich overnight. They didn't sign a record deal, get discovered and put into a TV sitcom or star in a movie, nor did they sign a multi-million-dollar contract to play ball for some professional sports team. They didn't work "get-rich-quick schemes" to make their money, but worked steadily and meticulously during their working years to build a solid financial foundation for themselves and their families.

The truth is that the overnight millionaire is often the overnight pauper. Stories have been done on lottery winners who made millions overnight, but lost it all in just a few years. As the book of Proverbs says:

An inheritance quickly gained at the beginning
will not be blessed at the end.

PROVERBS 20:21 NIV

and

> **Wealth [not earned but] won in haste or unjustly or from**
> **the production of things for vain or detrimental use**
> **[such riches] will dwindle away, but he who gathers**
> **little by little will increase [his riches].**

PROVERBS 13:11 AMP

In other words, most of America's wealthy did not get rich overnight, but built their wealth over the years. Whether they knew about it or not, and whether they were Christians or not, they worked the Storehouse Principle diligently throughout all of their lives. They made the choice to *be* financially independent and secure rather than to just *look* wealthy, and use savings, patience, and stewardship to obtain that goal. Money had no rule over them; instead they told their money what to do and it served them to build financial security and peace for their families despite the flow of the economic tides.

The Results Are Multiplied!

If you look at the tenets of another financial success classic, *The Richest Man in Babylon*, you will see that the principles in it are the same: Save your surplus, put them to work for yourself, don't "eat" your profits, and let them grow untouched. If you do this consistently over the years, financial stability and peace like you have never imagined will overtake you and your latter days will be far better than your former ones. In contrast, those who don't follow these principles will find that they have spent their security during their "former days," so they don't have any security in their "latter days." They will continue working beyond retirement, not because they want to, but because they have to!

It is important to understand that many successful people did this without directly relying on God. For too many of them, their wealth and financial peace here on earth is all they will ever have. But we are not without God! What I have seen is that when you do these things in obedience to God's principles, the results are multiplied! The Storehouse Principle is no get-rich-quick scheme, but it is also much different than simply a lifetime of scrimping and saving to build your wealth.

What I want you to see from the examples in these books is that these people have delivered themselves from the "buy now on credit" mentality of our world system and have thus stumbled into the storehouse blessing through the back door. They managed to make money their servant rather than serving it through self-discipline and willpower. How much more should we be able to do the same thing through the fruit of the Spirit and with the wisdom and power of God operating in our lives?

Another thing I have found interesting is that even financial books that are not of a Christian orientation talk about giving. Some even say that there is a spiritual aspect to philanthropy that will keep a cycle of blessing flowing in a person's life and help keep money in its proper perspective. They have discovered a godly spiritual principle, but they have just not discovered its Source yet! Being a blessing is part of being blessed!

Am I Tithing, or Is This the Jesus Lottery?

I do want to say one more thing about giving before we go on. Some sincere, but misguided, believers have equated tithing and giving with some kind of a get-rich-quick scheme, and give to the church expecting that someone, somehow will come in the next week and dump a million dollars on their doorsteps. Our giving is not a matter of buying tickets in the "Jesus lottery," in the hope that someday our ticket number will be picked and then the blessings will flow in! One of the main problems with this mentality is that it tends to ignore the blessings that may come in the form of ideas, opportunities, or any of a number of other things that are financial blessings, but may seem less spectacular than having an angel show up on our doorstep with a Publishers Clearing House® sweepstakes check! God is more pleased with our obedient giving than with our sacrificial giving. It was this type of thing that got Saul rejected as king of Israel! He thought he could disobey God's command to destroy all of the wealth and livestock of Israel's enemies, and keep some of the plunder for himself and for his country—and then make it up to God with sacrifices later. Samuel straightened him out, however:

> **Does the LORD delight in burnt offerings and sacrifices**
> **as much as in obeying the voice of the LORD?**
> **To obey is better than sacrifice,**
> **and to heed is better than the fat of rams.**

1 SAMUEL 15:22 NIV

I have even seen families give all of their money away to a traveling minister who inspired them, so that the next week they had to go back to the church to ask for help so that they could pay their mortgages! This is exactly the type of thing Paul was speaking about when he said:

> **If anyone does not provide for his relatives,**
> **and especially for his immediate family, he has denied the**
> **faith and is worse than an unbeliever.**

1 TIMOTHY 5:8 NIV

Yes, it is true that the love of money and the lust for other things can even corrupt our giving. As always, we need to have pure hearts before we can ever hope to handle money correctly. God loves a cheerful giver, not a selfish one!

What is influencing how you handle your money? Wisdom and God's guidance, or lust for deceitful riches and covetousness for what your neighbors have sitting in front of their house? Do we want the stuff, or the security and peace of having money in the bank? In a culture that, on average, spends more than its average income every year, we can't have both. We either have to choose to have a storehouse or the stuff, at least in the beginning. Then, once we have demonstrated the self-control that stewardship requires to put God first in all things, other blessings may flow to us as well; or He may put on our hearts a greater purpose for our money than we have ever imagined. If we are willing to be content with what we have now, and if we are willing to trust His leading and His timing, God can multiply what we have so that we will be a blessing not only to our families, but also to our churches, our communities, and the world. This is all part of the storehouse mentality that God wants to be part of us as we operate in His Storehouse Principle.

14

THE STOREHOUSE MENTALITY

*We want each of you to show this same diligence to
the very end, in order to make your hope sure.
We do not want you to become lazy, but to imitate
those who through faith and patience inherit what
has been promised.*

HEBREWS 6:11-12 NIV

The night after Pastor Al and I met to start this book, we went out to a Tex-Mex restaurant to eat with some friends. They appeared to be repaving the parking lot and a big section of it was torn up and littered with rubble from the work of the bulldozers that day. Because the parking lot was so full, we had to park near the torn up area. When we finished dinner and were getting ready to pull out to leave, Al touched me on the shoulder and said, "Hang on a minute." The way he said it, I thought he had forgotten something in the restaurant.

Al unbuckled his seatbelt, opened the door, and stepped out of the car. He crossed into the torn up area of the parking lot and stooped down in the dark to pick something up. From the light of a nearby streetlamp I caught a glint of it: it was the unmistakable sparkle you see several times a day from the copper of a penny.

As Al climbed back into the car, I said, "You made me stop just to pick up a penny? I thought you'd forgotten something! Why all the fuss over a penny! You have enough money already, don't you? Picking up pennies isn't going to make you rich!"

"Van," Al responded, "it's not about the penny. 'He that is faithful in least will be faithful in much.' It is about being faithful in little things. I think the way we usually blow it is that we are not faithful in the little things. Other ministers have told me that God has dealt with them in the same way. Picking up pennies is just a way of reminding me to be faithful in the little things."

As he said this, I remembered a story that someone had once told me about Sam Walton, the man who founded Wal-Mart. As some executives in the corporation were waiting to meet with him, someone mentioned Sam's habit of picking up small coins. As a test, one of the men dropped a nickel on the ground under the table, making sure it was only barely visible, to see what would happen. Sure enough, when Sam Walton walked into the room he greeted them all cordially, stooped down to pick up the nickel, and then sat down to start their meeting. That story had never made sense until Al shared this principle with me.

Benjamin Franklin said, "A penny saved, is a penny earned." That is no longer true, because there was no income tax in Franklin's day. Today, "A penny saved is worth more than a penny earned!" In other words, time spent saving money makes us more in the long run than time spent earning the same amount of money. You don't build financial peace just because you earn a lot of money—it is the money you keep that counts!

Systematically Activate It

To me, this "being faithful in little things" is what stewardship is all about. It is taking care of the little details many wouldn't bother with and applying biblical economic principles in *everything* that we do and not just when it is convenient. It is the diligence that looks at what we have, says it is enough, and uses wisdom and patience to get needed things at the best prices possible and waits for the luxuries until the time is right. This kind of resourcefulness is what I have seen in those who operate in the Storehouse Principle. It has also developed in my own life as I have put its tenets to work for my family and our business and ministry. As Jesus said:

> **"To those who use well what they are given, even more will be given. But from those who are unfaithful, even what little they have will be taken away."**
>
> LUKE 19:26 NLT

The difference between success and failure is often in the diligence in handling the small details.

A Simpler Word for Diligence Is Work

As Pastor Al mentioned in a previous chapter, when Solomon wanted to give an example of true diligence, he went to one of the smallest creatures around—the ant:

> Go to the ant, you sluggard;
> consider its ways and be wise!
>
> It has no commander,
> no overseer or ruler,
>
> yet it stores its provisions in summer
> and gathers its food at harvest.
>
> How long will you lie there, you sluggard?
> When will you get up from your sleep?
>
> A little sleep, a little slumber,
> a little folding of the hands to rest—
>
> and poverty will come on you like a bandit
> and scarcity like an armed man.
>
> PROVERBS 6:6-11 NIV

Solomon doesn't mince words. People who need to be supervised all of the time and cut corners when they can are *sluggards*—lazy people. If they are not diligent at work, then they will not be diligent at home either. If they are not diligent in spending other people's money, then they will not be diligent in spending—or saving—their own. As Jesus said:

And if you have not been trustworthy with someone else's
property, who will give you property of your own?

LUKE 16:12 NIV

The Message Bible paraphrases this passage this way:

If you're honest in small things,
you'll be honest in big things;
If you're a crook in small things,
you'll be a crook in big things.

If you're not honest in small jobs,
who will put you in charge of the store?

LUKE 16:11-12 THE MESSAGE

If you are going to apply the Storehouse Principle to your life, it
will take some diligence to change your present habits.

Be Faithful in Little Things

People like Pastor Jandl are not just diligent about picking up
pennies, but are faithful in the little things in all areas of their lives.
When he got the expensive desks that are now in the offices of his
church, many of their tops were covered with cigarette burn
marks—something that not only marred their appearance, but also
were not the things that you would want your church staff to sit
behind while dealing with the general public! So what did he do?
He pulled them out back and put everyone to work refinishing

them—hard work, indeed, but worth the savings for the value they got in the end.

He also contracted and built much of his present home himself—probably saving over $150,000 in the process. This was the same diligence and attention to detail that made him a quick riser through the ranks at the grocery chain where he worked, and has made everything that has to do with his ministry of the highest standard of excellence.

As I said before, the difference between success and failure is often in paying attention to the details that no one else cares to take care of. As Zig Ziglar says, "There is no traffic jam on the extra mile."

Diligence and Faithfulness Will Grow in Your Life

Living the Storehouse Principle requires this kind of diligence, but it also builds it, because carefully putting money away in your storehouse every paycheck is a small thing that in reality is no small accomplishment. It has a snowball effect to it, not only in how the money grows, but also in changing how you view money. Being faithful in this way is a level of diligence that is very uncommon among today's financial couch potatoes. But go to the ant for an example: little by little, and grain by grain, they build their anthills, tunnels, and colonies, and come rain, sleet, flood, or a long, hard winter, somehow they weather the storms because of their diligence to tend their storehouses.

Starting a storehouse and controlling our spending will take the same diligence. It may mean switching to buying everything with cash rather than on a credit card to keep from overspending each week. Or, it may mean going back to writing checks for each purchase and keeping your checkbook and accounts balanced. It may mean developing, implementing, and monitoring a budget. If you are financially out of shape now, it will take some diligent work to form new, healthier financial habits, regardless of how God specifically leads you to carry out the plan.

We are not in it alone, though. God has provided us with wisdom in His Word to keep our finances from taking over our lives. "Entering into His joy" means operating in the principles of the Bible as faithful and wise stewards.[1]

True Financial Freedom

Many who think they are doing great things for God will be very surprised when they get to heaven and God calls for an accounting of their stewardship and all they have to show for it is a big house, fancy cars, and the stuff they still owe money on. Certainly these can be blessings from God, but not if they are all that we have to show for our stewardship, or if they bring us continual financial pressure or strife in our marriages.

---

[1] See Matthew 24:45-51.

One of the most amazing discoveries in searching the Bible for what it says about money is that the pressure to keep up with other people—which is rooted in pride—has lost power over my wife and me the more we have deposited into our storehouse accounts. Where we had felt the constant pressure of paying our bills before, hope began to grow for our future as our financial base became more solid. As our storehouse grew, we began to look for ways to increase that growth, and Doni and I began cutting away the fat from our spending. We stopped looking at what others had as a determining factor of what our standard of living should be. If we wanted to buy something new, we would start saving up for it rather than raiding our storehouse or going into debt to buy it. More often than not, we ended up deciding we didn't really want it as much as we had thought in the first place. We decided to determine our own standard of living based on how God told us to live, regardless of whether we could afford more. We began to pay attention to the little things so that we could be faithful in them rather than just spending and hoping it would all work itself out when the credit card statements came in.

Living off of the Top of the Barrel

Pastor John Osteen, who was a close friend of Pastor Jandl and had a church near him in Houston, Texas, used to say it this way: "At Lakewood Church we pray for money when the barrel gets down to the top. It takes as much faith to believe God for a miracle on the bottom of the barrel as it does to use it to fill up the barrel. We have determined to live off of the top. It is like with milk in a pail: we live off of the cream that rises to the top and just leave the milk in there." In other words, they left their money in their storehouse until it was full and didn't touch it unless it was absolutely necessary. They prayed for money to cover extra expenses while maintaining *a full storehouse*. Their mentality was to live always off of their present cash flow and let their storehouses build for stability. Because of that, even though Pastor Osteen passed away a few years ago, his church is going stronger than ever now under his son Joel's leadership. His storehouse mentality of being faithful in the little things and making money his servant rather than mastering him created that stability.

The Storehouse Mentality

If I were going to sum up some of the attributes of "storehouse people" who believe and act upon the Storehouse Principle, people like Pastor Jandl, I would list them as follows:

1. Those with a storehouse mentality understand the true nature of money: that it is a force to be directed to create good and is not something to let guide our lives. Money is a tool, not a goal.

2. To them, stability and peace are more important than stuff. They live well below their means. They are cash flow conscious. Patience and self-control dictate what they buy, not

their wants, desires, and the attractiveness of something to their eyes. They would rather live without than buy on credit.

3. They are resourceful. They use what they have to meet their needs and desires and don't look to what their neighbor has. If they don't have the finances, then they use their talents or time. They are problem-solvers.

4. They understand the value of work and the value of a dollar. They work smart as well as hard. They also balance family, work, friends, and ministry quite well.

5. They have developed a knack for finding incredible bargains. They don't always have to pay full price for everything.

6. They find their contentment and satisfaction in life in following their God-given dreams, not in acquiring stuff— although, in fact, they often have very nice stuff. They are after true, not temporal, riches.

7. They work to learn more than to earn a paycheck. Then they take that knowledge and turn it into profits. In other words, they invest their time, rather than just their money. They find hobbies that help them grow personally and financially.

8. They are not interested in getting rich quick, but at the same time build their wealth in almost everything that they do. Like the ant, they are self-directed and build one grain at a time.

9. They are not, as they say in Texas, "Big hat, no cattle" people. They are not concerned with appearances. Many of them do not appear outwardly wealthy, though they may have millions in the bank.

10. They live to give, but they don't give to live. They know giving means both within their families and outside their families as well. They build for their children's and grandchildren's futures as well as that of their church and the ministries, charities, and nonprofit organizations they believe in. They understand that charity may not start at home, but it is part of it. They understand that they are blessed so that they can be a blessing.

Though these are just the tip of the iceberg, they are some of the most significant things that I have seen God building in our lives as Doni and I have put the Storehouse Principle into practice. If you will start your storehouse today, God will do the same for you. God has more blessings for you and yours than you have ever imagined. You only need to believe and act upon the Storehouse Principle.

A Closing Message from Al and Van

PART THREE

PUTTING IT ALL TOGETHER:

LIVING OUT THE

STOREHOUSE BLESSING

15

ARE YOU A BLESSING?

> "I will make you a great nation;
> I will bless you
> And make your name great;
> And *you shall be a blessing.*
>
> "I will bless those who bless you,
> And I will curse him who curses you;
> And *in you all the families of the earth shall be blessed.*"

GENESIS 12:2-3 *(italics added)*

Why does God command a blessing on us in our storehouses? So that we can be blessed, and be a blessing to others. God wants us to have liberty from serving money and putting in an inordinate amount of time worrying about getting more money. He wants us to have time to be with our families, go to their events or games, be home to tuck them in at night and read to them, have time to contribute to our churches and communities, as well as have the resources to provide for loved ones and fulfill the dreams He has placed within each of us. God wants His intended blessings on us to be blessings in reality, and not to do more harm than good. He wants us to radiate in the glow of His blessings in such a way that others are drawn to Him through us.

The Storehouse Principle and the other biblical guidelines we have looked at in this book are for just that: to open you up to the blessings of God so that you can be a blessing to others. How exactly does it work? You can try to rationalize it in your mind and say that these principles are just good common sense and sound money management, but our experience, and that of others who have heard about this principle from us and put it into practice, says that it is much more. Starting a storehouse has not changed the way we manage money so much as it has changed the way we view life—our time, our talents, and our treasures. It has also changed the way we view ourselves: we are no longer victims of what the world would do to us, but are victors—people of self-control, discipline, and the resources to make a difference.

God Wants to Bless You like He Blessed Abraham

Just as God blessed Abraham so that Abraham would be a blessing to the world, God wants to bless us. But there was a good deal that Abraham had to learn before God could bless him so abundantly. God had to get him to see himself as the father and blesser of many nations, which is one of the reasons God changed his name from simply Abram ("father") to Abraham ("father of a multitude"). It is also why He made a covenant with him in Genesis 17 and led him step-by-step for twenty-five years before His promise to him was fulfilled and Isaac was born. God had to first change Abraham's heart and develop his faith so that he could receive the promise.

God wants to do the same thing with each one of us. It is unlikely that this book has fallen into your hands accidentally, because God wants to walk with you as He did with Abraham. In fact, because of the life and ministry of Jesus, we can have even a closer relationship with God than Abraham did. We aren't patriarchs of the faith as Abraham was, but we have the blood of Jesus and the indwelling of the Holy Spirit, which weren't available to Abraham. Many of us "dedicate" our finances to God, but do we really walk with Him daily, praying over our daily decisions, purchases, and offerings? The fact is, because much of the teaching about our relationship to money can be so confusing, many of us are too ashamed or too afraid to let Jesus be Lord of our checkbooks in the same way that He is in other areas of our lives. We think dealing with money is not spiritual enough to involve Him. Yet after reading what Jesus taught about money, we see that He wants to be involved in every single area of our lives, including our financial life. In fact, that is exactly one of the things that got Israel into trouble before Jesus came into this world: Israel had not kept God on the throne in the management of their finances, but, instead, allowed money to replace Him as their god. We in the American church seem in many ways to have let the same thing happen to us today. It is a trend that we need to reverse.

If we are going to trust God to direct our finances, we will have to obey His Word in how we manage them. Creating a storehouse is an easy first step in this, but building a storehouse while ignoring the rest of the wisdom in the Bible about handling money will leave us no better off then we were before—at some point, we'll just let some "lust of the eyes" consume our savings. If we are to operate according to God's economic system rather than that of the secular American culture, we cannot afford to ignore His wisdom in the area of financial management. God wants us to be influential people for good in the world, so we need to exercise His wisdom to get the financial wherewithal to do it. We can't help others with what we need for ourselves, only with what we are able to give.

But usually, changes don't happen overnight. God's promises tend to become real in our lives much more like a farm, with its seasons of seedtime and harvest, rather than like a supermarket with its instant purchases. We plant the seed of the promises of God in our heart, water it with the water of the Word, expose it to the light of the Son, and slowly, but steadily, it becomes real, tangible fruit in our lives. Of course, we prefer the supermarket model with the instant gratification and the immense variety. God doesn't give us forty-one choices of cereal; He gives us one choice, obedience.

Dig into God's Word and get a proper understanding of what money really is and how we are to relate to it. In the meantime, you also need to start putting something aside in your storehouse every time you receive income—whether it's a set percentage or a fixed number of dollars every time is up to you—but you need to activate this principle in your life. Then leave that money in the storehouse and let it grow as God directs. As you grow in wisdom, apply that wisdom to the management of these finances and invest it properly to take care of the future.

Don't Let Fear Keep You from Starting a Storehouse

A major reason why many people don't manage their finances properly is fear. They are afraid to face up to their poor stewardship of the past and are afraid to face all of the needs of the future. It all seems too daunting. It seems easier to just appease your desires by buying the stuff you think will make you happy now while ignoring your responsibility to take care of the future. Spending and buying can actually become a form of medication for those who are afraid to change. But in the long run, that new big screen TV set is not going to put your kids through college or build for your retirement. We often think that we don't have enough to make a difference, but we miss the subtle power of obeying God and seeing Him work through little things to provide an increase over time.

> **Little by little I will drive them out before you, until you have increased enough to take possession of the land.**
>
> EXODUS 23:30 NIV

As God did with Abraham, He wants to walk each of us through the steps to become people through whom He can bless all the families of the earth. We need to do our part so that God can do His. Then you will experience what others who have begun living out the Storehouse Principle already discovered. God's part is not necessarily fast, but it accelerates as it goes along, and though the fruit of our obedience is not necessarily spectacular, it is still very supernatural. If we just obey God and do things His way, His blessings will overtake us beyond our wildest imagination. It is not that you will necessarily be spectacularly rich, but that you will never get to the end of His joy and financial peace by turning this crucial area of life over to His wisdom.

Being a Storehouse Blesser

We have to be willing to be blessed beyond our wildest expectations so that we can be a blessing beyond our wildest expectations. If we are willing to do that—to be modern-day Abrahams using our resources to further God's kingdom on the earth—then we must put ourselves into positions to be used of God in ways we have never before thought possible. We just have to step out in faith as Abraham did, obey God, and walk in His blessings.

> **Abraham believed God, and it was accounted to him
> for righteousness. Know ye therefore that they which are
> of faith, the same are the children of Abraham. And the
> scripture, foreseeing that God would justify the heathen
> through faith, preached before the gospel unto Abraham,
> saying, *In thee shall all nations be blessed. So then they
> which be of faith are blessed with faithful Abraham. . . .***

> Christ hath redeemed us from the curse of the law, being
> made a curse for us: for it is written, Cursed is every one
> that hangeth on a tree: *That the blessing of Abraham might*
> *come on the Gentiles through Jesus Christ; that we might*
> *receive the promise of the Spirit through faith.*

GALATIANS 3:6-9,13-14 *(italics added)*

God has given us the Storehouse Principle to make a way to provide for ourselves, our families, our churches, our communities, and our world. He blesses us so that we can have true rest from our labors and enjoy the things He has given us, and not so that we can have our peace and joy consumed by the stressful desire to constantly get more things. Here is what Solomon said about the love of money and its power over us:

> Whoever loves money never has money enough;
> whoever loves wealth is never satisfied
> with his income.
> This too is meaningless.
>
> As goods increase,
> so do those who consume them.
> And what benefit are they to the owner
> except to feast his eyes on them?
>
> The sleep of a laborer is sweet,
> whether he eats little or much,
> but the abundance of a rich man
> permits him no sleep.

I have seen a grievous evil under the sun:
wealth hoarded to the harm of its owner,

or wealth lost through some misfortune,
so that when he has a son
there is nothing left for him.

Naked a man comes from his mother's womb,
and as he comes, so he departs.
He takes nothing from his labor
that he can carry in his hand.

This too is a grievous evil:
As a man comes, so he departs,
and what does he gain,
since he toils for the wind?

ECCLESIASTES 5:10-16 NIV *(italics added)*

It is possible to gather wealth and have it be meaningless—or even worse, it might draw us away from God—but those who have a proper attitude toward money can use it to ease tensions caused by lack and to provide a sense of stability instead:

Then I realized that it is good and proper for a man to eat and
drink, and to find satisfaction in his toilsome labor under
the sun during the few days of life God has given him—for
this is his lot. Moreover, when God gives any man wealth and
possessions, and enables him to enjoy them, to accept his
lot and be happy in his work—*this is a gift of God. He seldom*
reflects on the days of his life, because God keeps him
occupied with gladness of heart.

ECCLESIASTES 5:18-20 NIV *(italics added)*

People who have more than they need can sleep soundly knowing that God is their helper and their strength. They rest assured knowing God has blessed them with more than enough resources to fulfill God's dreams for their lives. They "seldom reflect on the days of their life," meaning that they don't spend much time being concerned with their financial situation or other woes—they have more time to think of others. God gives such people a place of rest and refreshment from struggling too hard in order to provide for themselves and their families. With these things secured and established, like a house built firmly on a rock, they know that they can weather life's storms as well as help others to find the same peace and protection. They have a place of stability from which to reach out their hand to others and help them up onto the Rock as well.

Are we servants of God or servants of money? Are we a blessing on the earth? Are we living in the peace of God concerning our finances? If you find yourself responding negatively to any of these questions, then today is the day to pick up the Bible and start living it by "building" a storehouse.

God has a great blessing He would like to bestow on your family and your world through *you*. Today is the day to start being that blessing. Put the Storehouse Principle to work in your life, let God give you extraordinary financial stability, and get ready to be a greater blessing to your world than you ever thought possible.

In the next chapter, you'll find four people who didn't know why, how or where to start, but trusted God "that there must be a better way," and found a simple answer to some of life's most complex problems: The Storehouse Principle, a revolutionary God idea for creating extraordinary financial peace in their lives!

16

NO LONGER A VICTIM

God shows no partiality.

ACTS 10:34 NKJV

The Storehouse Principle may sound amazing to some of you. If it's unique to the two of us, however, and is only meant for us, then it won't be of any benefit to you. But the Storehouse Principle is for everybody. Here are testimonies from four friends who learned about the Storehouse Principle and have seen it work in their lives, as well:

Pastor Tim Brooks' Story

As long as I live, I will never forget the day I sat in my office pouring out my heart to Al Jandl about my financial problems. It was a crisp, clear day in the fall of 1988 at about 3:00 in the afternoon. I sat at my desk and Al sat across from me. At the time, if I didn't get $50,000 by the Friday of that week, I was going under. I needed a financial miracle. I was working myself into a sweat, unable to stop talking. Al sat there listening kindly without saying a word.

"I am serving God, Al. I have given my whole life to God—isn't He supposed to take care of me? I'm tithing—I've never missed tithing.

I go to church every time the doors are open. I am doing the best I can and I don't have any money. I can't make ends meet. I am fighting it day in and day out. I never have any money—I've never had any money. I feel as if I am always drinking Pepto-Bismol with a knot in my stomach because I worry so much about paying the next set of bills. Is this how I am supposed to live serving God?

"I am not a lazy man, Al. I have worked hard, long days all of my life! But no matter how hard I work, I still don't have any money! Jesus said that if we would seek His kingdom first, He would take care of all of these things, but it's not happening! It can't be me! Something just isn't right here!" I went on and on and on.

Al sat listening patiently. I knew he was a man of wisdom in finances and could help me, but he offered no advice. I don't know how long I went on, but I told him my troubles from top to bottom.

Finally, I took a breath. In that short gap, he said simply, "Do you want me to tell you? Or do you just want to talk about it?"

I couldn't believe his response, but, you know, a lot of times we don't want the answer, we just want to gripe. But I was tired of griping. I wanted to know the answer to my situation and get out of it, so I said, "Tell me what I need to do."

A Simple Answer to a Complex Problem

"Turn to Deuteronomy chapter 28."

I grabbed my Bible, and I opened it to Deuteronomy. I began to read along as Al quoted verses 1 through 7 to me out of his Bible. Then *he took a brief pause, looked up to make sure I was really listening, and read verse 8:*

The Lord shall command the blessing upon thee in thy storehouses, and in all that thou settest thine hand unto; and he shall bless thee in the land which the LORD thy God giveth thee.

Then he said, "There's your problem."

As I had sat listening to him read, my mind had taken off again trying to figure out how I was going to pay the electric company, make my car payment, and take care of all of the other bills that were coming due—I had more bills than he had time to hear about—and this was his answer? I had to bring myself back to what he was saying, but I still didn't understand what he was talking about, so I just let him go on.

"You see, God commands a blessing on your storehouse. Do you have a storehouse? If you don't have a storehouse, then you have nothing for God to bless."

"What's a storehouse?" I asked.

"That's where you put your surplus—like in a savings account. Do you have a savings account? I don't mean just an account at the bank to back up your checking account, but an account you put extra money into every time you get paid. Then you leave it there. It is your extra, your reserve, your surplus. If you don't have a surplus, it doesn't make any sense for God to bless you. How can God responsibly bless anyone who consumes all they have week after week, month after month, and year after year?

God Will Not Bless Your Irresponsibility

"God commands a blessing on what you have extra—on what you responsibly save today to protect tomorrow. That is what storehouses were to the people in Deuteronomy—they saved from what they harvested today to eat until the next harvest and to plant the next season. God doesn't command a blessing on what you need, but on what you have. You have a need, because you have no reserves. From what you are saying, I can tell you spend more than you bring in. God is not going to bless someone for spending more than they have. If you gave one of your daughters a dollar bill, and she lost it, would you turn around and give her a hundred dollar bill? No, that would be irresponsible. You wouldn't give her more until she shows she can faithfully handle that smaller amount. God isn't irresponsible, so that is why He can't bless His children who don't faithfully handle their money either."

When he said that, it was as if a bomb went off inside of me.

For a moment, I couldn't speak. I suddenly saw for the first time what I had been missing that had allowed me to get into so much financial trouble. I realized that I was used to consuming everything that came through my hands every paycheck—and more, because I had bought so much on credit! In my lifetime I had made $20 a week and I had made as much as $200 a week—I realized that when I made $20, I spent $22; when I made $200, I spent $225. I had always consumed more than I made and had never had any extra. Yet, despite that, I knew that even I wouldn't bless my daughters if they did that, because the more money I gave them, the further they would dig themselves into debt—just as I had! That revelation was like a rock had smashed through glass in my soul—I instantly understood what I had done wrong all of these years. But where did that lead me? Even if I changed right away, I still had no extra money to start a store-house account with! Sure, this was a tremendous insight, but what was I going to do to get myself out of trouble that week?

That's Great—But I Need Money to Pay My Bills Today!

So I found my tongue again and said, "This is a great teaching, but I can't pay my bills right now. I can't afford to start a storehouse now! Are you saying I should start putting money in a savings account now when I can't even afford to pay my electric bill? Is that what you are telling me? I can't afford a savings account."

"Tim, that is exactly what I am telling you. I can't explain it and I am not here to argue with you. If you will do it, though, God will get involved in your finances as He never has before. If you don't, you will continue to live in need your whole life."

Somehow, inside of me, though I couldn't figure it out in my head, I knew what he was saying was true. I made the commitment right at that moment that I would never, ever again earn another paycheck that I didn't put at least a few dollars into an account we had set up as a storehouse.

A Heartfelt Decision to Change

So the next day—I am talking about the very next day—after we said good-bye to Al as he left to return home, I put my wife and my *two daughters in the car and told them, "We are going to the bank, and everybody here is opening up a savings account." On the way, I told my family about what a storehouse was and why we all needed to have one. When I got to the bank, I opened a storehouse account for both of my girls, my wife and me, our church, and our business— I opened a storehouse account for everything I could think of to open an account for!*

Since that day, over fifteen years ago, neither my ministry nor my family has had any money that came into our hands that we didn't tithe on first and then put some of it into a storehouse.

And, since that day, over fifteen years ago, neither my ministry nor my family has needed another financial miracle. Our bills are all paid, and we have always had money left over.

Today Tim's ministry and family are continuing to thrive. He was living in a trailer when Al met with him all those years ago, and today he and his family live in a nice home with the mortgage completely paid off. His children, like ours, understand the Storehouse Principle and are using it to build firm foundations for themselves and their families.

A Letter from Dwayne Sheriff

In the early days of pulling this book together, Al also received the following letter from another friend with whom he had shared the Storehouse Principle—a man he has come to respect as one of the most thorough and inspiring Bible teachers he has ever met. Here is his story, in his own words:

In what seemed from the outside like a "chance meeting" ended up being a divine appointment from God that impacted my ministry and changed my life completely in the area of finances. While picking my son up from Brookhill camp several years ago, I was allowed to sit in on a meeting between Al Jandl and Tim Brooks. I had never met Pastor Jandl before that day; however, as he began sharing some simple truths concerning God's Storehouse Principle, my spirit leaped within me and I knew I had to know more.

Pouring myself into the Word concerning the Storehouse Principle, God began revealing His truths to me in a powerful way. After having the privilege of sitting down with Pastor Jandl again, I gained confirmation and clarity on God commanding His blessing on the storehouses. Immediately, I began putting this principle into operation in our ministry and our home. God is always faithful and His Word is true. Our finances for the ministry, and personally, experienced a major turnaround. They continue to do so as we are faithful to build storehouses and are good stewards in God's kingdom.

To date, our ministry has distributed over four million cassette teaching tapes absolutely free. Presently, distribution of free tapes runs between sixty thousand and seventy thousand tapes per month. As one can imagine, I must believe for supernatural finances in order to meet the present and ever-expanding need. Without the Storehouse Principle, and God's blessing on good stewardship and faithfulness,

*this would not be possible. I have also been able to share this princi-
ple with many others who have taken hold of this truth and seen a
turnaround in their finances as well.*

*God does not bless gimmicks, schemes, and "get rich overnight"
propaganda that many are buying into. God blesses faithfulness in
the little things and will make us rulers of much. The Storehouse
Principle and the disciplined exercise in stewardship and faithfulness
in the riches of this world prepare us to handle the true riches (i.e.,
spiritual things—Luke chapters 16 and 19). People at large do not
have a financial problem; they have a stewardship, discipline, and
faithfulness problem. The Storehouse Principle may seem natural,
but is very spiritual and supernatural. I thank God for my good
friend, Al Jandl, and his willingness to share this truth with me.*

Thanks again!

Your Friend, Duane Sheriff

A Letter from Knoxville, Tennessee

This testimony came to us from a single mother in Knoxville,
Tennessee who heard Van preach on the Storehouse Principle a couple of years ago:

*Reverend Van Crouch comes regularly to minister at my church,
the Knoxville Christian Center in Knoxville, Tennessee. Since I serve
on the staff at the church as the Promotions Director for our
Christian concerts and special events, I have had the chance to meet
with Reverend Crouch and his lovely wife, Doni, on several different*

occasions. I have always appreciated his marvelous sense of humor and the timeliness of the messages God gives him to share with us.

I am a single mom of three children and have never received a dime of child support. Although I was earning a good salary at the job I used to have, I felt prompted to take a church staff position so that I could spend more time with my children. Yet, no matter how much money we had, we always seemed to be living from urgent need to urgent need. Because of this, we often had to put off buying things we needed. When a need arose for new tires for our car, I could never afford to buy more than one tire at a time. If the car broke down coming home from work, I would walk home in the rain rather than take a ride from a stranger. If we ever wanted to take a vacation, which was generally an inexpensive camping trip, we would always have to have a garage sale first to be able to have enough money to go.

I have struggled with my finances and never seem to have enough. Yet I know God is faithful, so I have always tithed and given offerings in obedience to scripture as well as volunteered some of my extra time to serve in our church. Through all this, though, the question "Why am I not prospering in my finances?" has always been in the back of my mind.

Then about eighteen months ago when he came for another visit, Reverend Crouch preached on the Storehouse Principle. The minute he started sharing this principle, I knew it was the missing link. I knew what I needed was the commanded blessing of God on my storehouses, a supernaturally empowered breakthrough to increase.

So that same week, I determined to start a storehouse savings account, then add ten percent of every check to it every time I got paid. I didn't back off my tithing or offerings, either. Suddenly I found my faith and hope rising as my storehouse began to grow. Less than a year later, I was able to buy four new tires at one time for our car and my children and I flew to Florida for a week's vacation! More importantly, though, something changed on the inside of me—I don't feel like a victim anymore.

About six months ago I decided to go to a county property tax sale to learn how to invest and make money. The prices for many of the properties were so low that I found myself bidding on a particularly attractive property on a main thoroughfare in our city. When I went to register my bid at $2,500.00, the clerk was amazed and asked how I had been able to buy that particular building. It appears that the city owned the adjacent property and had been planning to buy this one for some time. The clerk whispered to me, "You hold onto that property, honey. The city will buy it someday for a lot of money."

More recently I decided to make an offer to buy a day care facility. It's located next to one of the best elementary schools in the city and between two churches—an area ripe with clientele. This was born out of my daughter's dream to teach and train children through a day care system and so she could continue to be with her young children. I also thought that it could help others in my family with salaries and child care as well as provide quality Christian-oriented child care for those in our area that wanted it.

After two short years, I'm a new person on the inside. I'm on offense and no longer on defense in my finances. I feel secure and confident. I've always wanted to be a bigger player in building the Kingdom of God and now I'm prepared to live and to give!

Nancy Jenkins (Knoxville, Tennessee)

A Testimony from Rich Gradel

This testimony came from a pastor in Broken Arrow, Oklahoma:

I first heard about the Storehouse Principle from Van Crouch in 2003. Van shared with me about the difference it has made in his life and ministry, and about the positive reception from other people as he has shared it with them.

As an attorney, Certified Public Accountant, Certified Financial Planner, and now as pastor of New Beginnings Family Church in Broken Arrow, Oklahoma, I recognize that the Storehouse Principle is what many of my most successful clients have lived and what I dearly want the members of my flock to apply in their own lives.

Having searched the Scriptures for myself, I'm convinced that the application of the Storehouse Principle will revolutionize the church, individuals, families, communities, even governments. This is a balanced, accurate approach to "prosperity" that is supported by the will of God as expressed in His Word. It will produce a "comfort level" with success, without the worship of money; real prosperity, without greed or materialism; a holy walk with God rooted in pure motives and a readiness to be used by our Lord and Master. "Storehouse People" will have two essential ingredients of success: a lifestyle of self control and a habit of saving—in a word, "discipline," which is what is expected of a disciple of Jesus Christ.

I believe that God is speaking the "Storehouse" message to His people today to prepare us for coming events. Today's world is not the same as it used to be. It is now common for people to change jobs many times during their adult lives. Millions of middle-class Americans are one layoff or medical emergency away from bankruptcy. Many are fearful because of this financial uncertainty. By building store-houses, we can dispel that fear.

My wife, Donna, and I are committed to apply the Storehouse Principle in our own lives. I am already witnessing remarkable progress in the lives of our church members who have now heard this message—and not just in financial matters.

The Storehouse Principle is a practical way to revolutionize our walk with God. As much as some of us would like to do it, we cannot ignore the subject of money. If we keep our finances off limits to God, we will never be truly submitted to Him. If we allow Him to be Lord over our gathering, spending, and saving, we will please the Master of our stewardship. Why let a little thing like money interfere with our relationship with God?

I look forward to volumes of testimonies about how the Storehouse Principle has improved the spiritual and financial lives of "Storehouse People" who have put it into practice—including yours and mine!

Rich Gradel, Pastor (New Beginnings Family Church)

Now We Know What You Are Probably Thinking

As we have taught this principle to people over the years, we have seen three groups of responses.

The first group says, "I can't afford to pay my bills now! How am I supposed to start a storehouse! There is no way. This is too crazy." Or, they will try to reason it out in their minds—"Well, if you put ten dollars in the savings account—they are not paying but one or two percent interest right now—how is that ever going to make me any money?" And the people in this group will go on living as they do now—paycheck to paycheck, or perhaps even soon to be bankrupt—for the rest of their lives.

The second group will rush out and start a storehouse account today. For a few months they will diligently put away a little of every dollar that comes through their hands. Then, one day, they will see something that they have to have, or be invited on a trip somewhere with a group of friends, and they will go and get that money and blow it all. They may start again soon after that, but will eventually see having such a storehouse as pointless because no matter how diligent they are in saving, they still never amass enough to give them peace about their financial future—they always end up blowing it on something they want to have or do.

But there is a third group who will go out and apply this principle, and in a year from now—two years from now, five years from now, maybe even ten years from now—they are going to be exploding with the blessing of God, because God commands His blessing on their storehouses.

A minister we know used to always say, "Many people miss the supernatural because they are looking for the spectacular." We have to admit that what has happened to us is pretty spectacular and our financial blessings have definitely been miraculous. We know God can do the same for you, but not if you focus only on the blessings. There would be no point in both of us getting together to write this book for you if everything that has happened to us was because of some chance blessing of God. What you need to see is that by applying God's wisdom in our lives, we were in a place to receive God's blessings and make them last. And the same thing will happen to you if you put this principle into practice in your life. There are people we know who have been much more blessed than we have, and yet today they have nothing to show for it. The fact of the matter is that if you apply the Storehouse Principle to your life and never receive more than your regular salary, the wisdom of God can still turn it into incredible financial stability for you and your family. The key is to get God's wisdom just as Tim Brooks, Dwayne Sheriff, Nancy Jenkins and Rich Gradel have, and then when the blessings come, you will know how to make them a blessing for generations!

Now it's time for you to get started on your Storehouse adventure. You've traveled with us and heard about our journey and how God has transformed our lives, families and finances, but the point of all of this is to encourage you to believe God for yourself and begin to act on His promises and receive His commanded blessings on your life.

There's an old saying that "God can do more in ten seconds than we can do in ten years." We should never underestimate the power of prayer, the Word, and simple faith. In the final chapters, we've included a prayer for you to get started. You can pray this prayer once or every day, however the Lord leads you. After that you'll find some scriptures to help you renew your mind to God's Word.

God bless you as you love Him with all of your heart, soul and mind, and live and proclaim that Jesus is Lord!

17

BEGIN TO PRAY OVER YOUR FINANCES

The Storehouse Prayer

Dear Father God,

Thank You for Your goodness in providing for my financial needs. I dedicate every penny that comes into my home to You and to the furtherance of Your kingdom. Please help me to be a wise steward of the money that You have given me, so that I can give, meet my obligations, and put money into a storehouse savings program. I believe, according to Your Word in Deuteronomy 28:8, that You will command a blessing on the money that I save, the money that I give, and all the work that I put forth my hand to do.

I declare that Jesus is Lord over my finances, and I give the worry of financial pressure over to You, Father. Help me to be financially stable so that I can be a blessing to others. Thank You for giving me favor with You and with man, favor that surrounds me like a shield.

Thank You for Your Holy Spirit who lives in me. I believe that He will teach me how to manage my money and lead and guide me to the opportunities that would be a blessing, and warn me to stay away from people and situations that are not healthy financially. Thank You for helping me to live within my means, and to put away selfish desires to spend money needlessly on things that I could do without, or should delay buying until later.

I understand from Your Word, that the borrower is servant to the lender. Please help me to pay off any unnecessary debt as quickly as possible, and to not incur future debt. Help me to be careful of greed in every form, for I understand that a person's life does not consist of the possessions they own. Help me to be content with my current situation, so that I do not envy other people's wealth, nor covet their things or lifestyles.

Because You nurture and take care of every living thing, I know You will provide for my needs, so I will not worry about anything that may happen to me tomorrow, but I will focus on what You are teaching me today, and how I can be a blessing to others now.

I will bring my financial life into line with what You command and desire, regardless of personal desires and no matter what it takes. Help me to remember that the Storehouse Principle is not just about money, or things, but about obedience to Your Word and Your Spirit. I know that even the money that I have in savings is Your money Father; I am just a temporary steward of it. I do not trust in riches or things, but in You alone Lord. You have blessed me, so that I can be a blessing to others.

I pray these things in Jesus' name. Amen

The Eternal Security Prayer

**He is no fool who gives what he cannot keep
to gain what he cannot lose.**

JIM ELLIOT

No discussion on money or treasure would be complete without declaring that, in the end the only treasure that really matters is spiritual treasure. Our lives on earth are so short in comparison with eternal life, that our financial retirement plan is meaningless without eternal security. Jesus said:

For what is a man profited, if he shall gain the whole world, and lose his own soul? or what shall a man give in exchange for his soul?

MATTHEW 16:26

If you feel as uncertain or unstable about your spiritual life as many do about their finances, then pray this prayer and it will bring you peace with God.

Heavenly Father,

Thank You for making a way for me to have a relationship with You;

I realize that I am a sinner and need forgiveness, and that I am hopelessly lost without You. Thank You for being a perfect Father;

I ask you Lord Jesus, to be my Savior and my Lord.

I believe that You died for me. I want to turn from my sins.

I repent and receive Your life in exchange for my sin.

I choose to trust and follow You as my Lord and my Savior.

I now invite You to come into my heart and life.

In Jesus' name. Amen.[1]

---

[1] This is just the starting point for your new life with God. To strengthen your faith and relationship with God you should begin to: 1. Talk with God everyday (this is called "prayer"). 2. Find a church where Jesus is sincerely worshiped. 3. Read the Bible as much as possible. 4. Live your new life with an evidence of concern and love for other people. 5. Tell others about Jesus as the Lord gives you opportunities.

18

A BLUEPRINT FOR CHANGE

**All scripture is inspired by God and profitable for teaching,
for reproof, for correction, for training in righteousness;**

**So that the man of God may be adequate, equipped for
every good work.**

2 TIMOTHY 3:16-17 NASB

Real change and transformation occur in your life as you renew
your mind to God's way of thinking and acting. As you plant the
"seed" of God's word in your heart, and "water" it with worship,
meditation, obedience and prayer, you will bear "fruit" in every area
of your life.

Meditating on the scripture verses below is a great way to start
the process of transformation today. As you study these in your own
bible, in the context of the entire scripture, the Holy Spirit will
write them on your heart.

For study purposes, the scripture verses are organized into three
separate categories: "Abundance"; "Giving"; and "Faith." The verses
in the first category demonstrate that God is a God of abundance
Who desires to bless you. The verses in the second category illus-

trate the importance of being an unselfish giver in God's plans for your finances. The verses in the final category are meant to stir up your faith in God, knowing that it takes faith for you to enter God's promised land of financial freedom.

Let God's word dwell richly in you!

ABUNDANCE

Genesis 1:26, 28 *And God said, Let us make man in our image, after our likeness: and let them have dominion over the fish of the sea, and over the fowl of the air, and over the cattle, and over all the earth, and over every creeping thing that creepeth upon the earth. . . . And God blessed them, and God said unto them, Be fruitful, and multiply, and replenish the earth, and subdue it: and have dominion over the fish of the sea, and over the fowl of the air, and over every living thing that moveth upon the earth.*

Genesis 12:3 *And I will bless them that bless thee, and curse him that curseth thee: and in thee shall all families of the earth be blessed.*

Genesis 13:2 *And Abram was very rich in cattle, in silver, and in gold.*

Genesis 15:1 *After these things the word of the Lord came unto Abram in a vision, saying, Fear not, Abram: I am thy shield, and thy exceeding great reward.*

Genesis 17:6 *And I will make thee exceeding fruitful, and I will make nations of thee, and kings shall come out of thee.*

Genesis 22:17-18 *That in blessing I will bless thee, and in multiplying I will multiply thy seed as the stars of the heaven, and as the sand which is upon the sea shore; and thy seed shall possess the gate of his enemies; And in thy seed shall all the nations of the earth be blessed; because thou hast obeyed my voice.*

Genesis 26:12 *Then Isaac sowed in that land, and received in the same year an hundredfold: and the Lord blessed him.*

Genesis 28:22 *And this stone, which I have set for a pillar, shall be God's house: and of all that thou shalt give me I will surely give the tenth unto thee.*

Genesis 39:3 *And his master saw that the Lord was with him, and that the Lord made all that he did to prosper in his hand.*

Exodus 23:25 *And ye shall serve the Lord your God, and he shall bless thy bread, and thy water; and I will take sickness away from the midst of thee.*

Leviticus 26:3-13 *If ye walk in my statutes, and keep my commandments, and do them; Then I will give you rain in due season, and the land shall yield her increase, and the trees of the field shall yield their fruit. And your threshing shall reach unto the vintage, and the vintage shall reach unto the sowing time: and ye shall eat your bread to the full, and dwell in your land safely. And I will give peace in the land, and ye shall lie down, and none shall make you afraid: and I will rid evil beasts out of the land, neither shall the sword go through your land. And ye shall chase your enemies, and they shall fall before you by the sword. And five of you shall chase an hundred, and an hundred of you shall put ten thousand to flight: and your enemies shall fall before you by the sword. For I will have respect unto you, and make you fruitful, and multiply you, and establish my covenant* *with you. And ye shall eat old store, and bring forth the old because of the new. And I will set my tabernacle among you: and my soul shall not abhor you. And I will walk among you, and will be your God, and ye shall be my people. I am the Lord your God, which brought you forth out of the land of Egypt, that ye should not be their bondmen; and I have broken the bands of your yoke, and made you go upright.*

Deuteronomy 8:18 *But thou shalt remember the LORD thy God: for it is he that giveth thee power to get wealth, that he may establish his covenant which he sware unto thy fathers, as it is this day.*

Deuteronomy 28:1-14 *And it shall come to pass, if thou shalt hearken diligently unto the voice of the LORD thy God, to observe and to do all his commandments which I command thee this day, that the LORD thy God will set thee on high above all nations of the earth: And all these blessings shall come on thee,*

and overtake thee, if thou shalt hearken unto the voice of the LORD thy God. Blessed shalt thou be in the city, and blessed shalt thou be in the field. Blessed shall be the fruit of thy body, and the fruit of thy ground, and the fruit of thy cattle, the increase of thy kine, and the flocks of thy sheep. Blessed shall be thy basket and thy store. Blessed shalt thou be when thou comest in, and blessed shalt thou be when thou goest out. The LORD shall cause thine enemies that rise up against thee to be smitten before thy face: they shall come out against thee one way, and flee before thee seven ways. The LORD shall command the blessing upon thee in thy storehouses, and in all that thou settest thine hand unto; and he shall bless thee in the land which the LORD thy God giveth thee. The LORD shall establish thee an holy people unto himself, as he hath sworn unto thee, if thou shalt keep the commandments of the LORD thy God, and walk in his

ways. And all people of the earth shall see that thou art called by the name of the LORD; and they shall be afraid of thee. And the LORD shall make thee plenteous in goods, in the fruit of thy body, and in the fruit of thy cattle, and in the fruit of thy ground, in the land which the LORD sware unto thy fathers to give thee. The LORD shall open unto thee his good treasure, the heaven to give the rain unto thy land in his season, and to bless all the work of thine hand: and thou shalt lend unto many nations, and thou shalt not borrow. And the LORD shall make thee the head, and not the tail; and thou shalt be above only, and thou shalt not be beneath; if that thou hearken unto the commandments of the LORD thy God, which I command thee this day, to observe and to do them: And thou shalt not go aside from any of the words which I command thee this day, to the right hand, or to the left, to go after other gods to serve them.

Deuteronomy 29:9 *Keep therefore the words of this covenant, and do them, that ye may prosper in all that ye do.*

Deuteronomy 30:9-10, 14-16 *And the LORD thy God will make thee plenteous in every work of thine hand, in the fruit of thy body, and in the fruit of thy cattle, and in the fruit of thy land, for good: for the LORD will again rejoice over thee for good, as he rejoiced over thy fathers: If thou shalt hearken unto the voice of the LORD thy God, to keep his commandments and his statutes which are written in this book of the law, and if thou turn unto the LORD thy God with all thine heart, and with all thy soul. . . .But the word is very nigh unto thee, in thy mouth, and in thy heart, that thou mayest do it. See, I have set before thee this day life and good, and death and evil; In that I command thee this day to love the LORD thy God, to walk in his ways, and to keep his commandments and his statutes*

and his judgments, that thou mayest live and multiply: and the LORD thy God shall bless thee in the land whither thou goest to possess it.

Joshua 1:8 *This book of the law shall not depart out of thy mouth; but thou shalt meditate therein day and night, that thou mayest observe to do according to all that is written therein: for then thou shalt make thy way prosperous, and then thou shalt have good success.*

1 Samuel 2:8 *He raiseth up the poor out of the dust, and lifteth up the beggar from the dunghill, to set them among princes, and to make them inherit the throne of glory: for the pillars of the earth are the LORD's, and he hath set the world upon them.*

1 Kings 2:3 *go the way of all the earth: be thou strong therefore, and shew thyself a man; And keep the charge of the LORD thy God, to walk in his ways, to keep his statutes, and his commandments, and his judgments, and his testimonies, as it is*

written in the law of Moses, that thou mayest prosper in all that thou doest, and whithersoever thou turnest thyself.

2 Chronicles 1:11-12 *And God said to Solomon, Because this was in thine heart, and thou hast not asked riches, wealth, or honour, nor the life of thine enemies, neither yet hast asked long life; but hast asked wisdom and knowledge for thyself, that thou mayest judge my people, over whom I have made thee king: Wisdom and knowledge is granted unto thee; and I will give thee riches, and wealth, and honor, such as none of the kings have had that have been before thee, neither shall there any after thee have the like.*

2 Chronicles 15:7 *Be ye strong therefore, and let not your hands be weak: for your work shall be rewarded.*

2 Chronicles 26:5 *And he sought God in the days of Zechariah, who had understanding in the visions of God: and as long as he sought the LORD, God made him to prosper.*

Job 42:12 So the Lord blessed the latter end of Job more than his beginning: for he had fourteen thousand sheep, and six thousand camels, and a thousand yoke of oxen, and a thousand she asses.

Psalms 1:1-3 Blessed is the man that walketh not in the counsel of the ungodly, nor standeth in the way of sinners, nor sitteth in the seat of the scornful. But his delight is in the law of the LORD; and in his law doth he meditate day and night. And he shall be like a tree planted by the rivers of water, that bringeth forth his fruit in his season; his leaf also shall not wither; and whatsoever he doeth shall prosper.

Psalms 23:1-2 The LORD is my shepherd; I shall not want. He maketh me to lie down in green pastures: he leadeth me beside the still waters.

Psalms 34:9-10 O fear the LORD, ye his saints: for there is no want to them that fear him. The young lions do lack, and suffer hunger: but they that seek the LORD shall not want any good thing.

Psalms 37:25 I have been young, and now am old; yet have I not seen the righteous forsaken, nor his seed begging bread.

Psalms 85:12 Yea, the LORD shall give that which is good; and our land shall yield her increase.

Psalms 103: 1-5 Bless the LORD, O my soul: and all that is within me, bless his holy name. Bless the LORD, O my soul, and forget not all his benefits: Who forgiveth all thine iniquities; who healeth all thy diseases; Who redeemeth thy life from destruction; who crowneth thee with lovingkindness and tender mercies; Who satisfieth thy mouth with good things; so that thy youth is renewed like the eagle's.

Psalms 105:37 He brought them forth also with silver and gold: and there was not one feeble person among their tribes.

Psalms 107:38 He blesseth them also, so that they are multiplied greatly; and suffereth not their cattle to decrease.

Psalms 112:1-3 Praise ye the LORD. Blessed is the man that feareth the LORD, that delighteth greatly in his commandments. His seed shall be mighty upon earth: the generation of the upright shall be blessed. Wealth and riches shall be in his house: and his righteousness endureth for ever.

Psalms 113:7-9 He raiseth up the poor out of the dust, and lifteth the needy out of the dunghill; That he may set him with princes, even with the princes of his people. He maketh the barren woman to keep house, and to be a joyful mother of children. Praise ye the LORD.

Proverbs 8:21 That I may cause those that love me to inherit substance; and I will fill their treasures.

Proverbs 10:3-4 The LORD will not suffer the soul of the righteous to famish: but he casteth away the substance of the wicked. He becometh poor that dealeth with a slack hand: but the hand of the diligent maketh rich.

Proverbs 10:22 The blessing of the LORD, it maketh rich, and he addeth no sorrow with it.

Proverbs 12:11 He that tilleth his land shall be satisfied with bread: but he that followeth vain persons is void of understanding.

Proverbs 13:22 A good man leaveth an inheritance to his children's children: and the wealth of the sinner is laid up for the just.

Proverbs 15:6 In the house of the righteous is much treasure: but in the revenues of the wicked is trouble.

Proverbs 22:7 The rich ruleth over the poor, and the borrower is servant to the lender.

Proverbs 28:20 A faithful man shall abound with blessings: but he that maketh haste to be rich shall not be innocent.

Ecclesiastes 5:19 Every man also to whom God hath given riches and wealth, and hath given him power to eat thereof, and to take his portion, and to rejoice in his labor; this is the gift of God.

Isaiah 1: 19 If ye be willing and obedient, ye shall eat the good of the land.

Isaiah 48:17 Thus saith the LORD, thy Redeemer, the Holy One of Israel; I am the LORD thy God which teacheth thee to profit, which leadeth thee by the way that thou shouldest go.

Joel 2:25 And I will restore to you the years that the locust hath eaten, the cankerworm, and the caterpiller, and the palmerworm, my great army which I sent among you.

Matthew 6:33 But seek ye first the kingdom of God, and his righteousness; and all these things shall be added unto you.

Matthew 7:7-11 Ask, and it shall be given you; seek, and ye shall find; knock, and it shall be opened unto you: For every one that asketh receiveth; and he that seeketh findeth; and to him that knocketh it shall be opened. Or what man is there of you, whom if his son ask bread, will he give him a stone? Or if he ask a fish, will he give him a serpent? If ye then, being evil, know how to give good gifts unto your children, how much more shall your Father which is in heaven give good things to them that ask him?

Mark 10:28-30 Then Peter began to say unto him, Lo, we have left all, and have followed thee. And Jesus answered and said, Verily I say unto you, There is no man that hath left house, or brethren, or sisters, or father, or mother, or wife, or children, or lands, for my sake, and the gospel's, But he shall receive an hundredfold now in this time, houses, and brethren, and sisters, and mothers, and children, and lands, with persecutions; and in the world to come eternal life.

Luke 12:31-34 But rather seek ye the kingdom of God; and all these things shall be added unto you. Fear not, little flock; for it is your Father's good pleasure to give you the kingdom. Sell that ye have, and give alms; provide yourselves bags which wax not old, a treasure in the heavens that faileth not, where no thief approacheth, neither moth corrupteth. For where your treasure is, there will your heart be also.

John 10:10 The thief cometh not, but for to steal, and to kill, and to destroy: I am come that they might have life, and that they might have it more abundantly.

Romans 8:32 He that spared not his own Son, but delivered him up for us all, how shall he not with him also freely give us all things?

2 Corinthians 8:7-9
Therefore, as ye abound in every thing, in faith, and utterance, and knowledge, and in all diligence, and in your love to us, see that ye abound in this grace also. I speak not by commandment, but by occasion of the forwardness of others, and to prove the sincerity of your love. For ye know the grace of our Lord Jesus Christ, that, though he was rich, yet for your sakes he became poor, that

ye through his poverty might be rich.

2 Corinthians 9:8-11
And God is able to make all grace abound toward you; that ye, always having all sufficiency in all things, may abound to every good work: (As it is written, He hath dispersed abroad; he hath given to the poor: his righteousness remaineth for ever. Now he that ministereth seed to the sower both minister bread for your food, and multiply your seed sown, and increase the fruits of your righteousness;) Being enriched in every thing to all bountifulness, which causeth through us thanksgiving to God.

1 Thessalonians 4:11-12
And that ye study to be quiet, and to do your own business, and to work with your own hands, as we commanded you; That ye may walk honestly toward them that are without, and that ye may have lack of nothing.

2 Thessalonians 3:10-14
For even when we were with you, this we com-

manded you, that if any would not work, neither should he eat. For we hear that there are some which walk among you disorderly, working not at all, but are busybodies. Now them that are such we command and exhort by our Lord Jesus Christ, that with quietness they work, and eat their own bread. But ye, brethren, be not weary in well doing. And if any man obey not our word by this epistle, note that man, and have no company with him, that he may be ashamed.

Galatians 3:29 And if ye be Christ's, then are ye Abraham's seed, and heirs according to the promise.

James 1:17 Every good gift and every perfect gift is from above, and cometh down from the Father of lights, with whom is no variableness, neither shadow of turning.

3 John 1:2 Beloved, I wish above all things that thou mayest prosper and be in health, even as thy soul prospereth.

GIVING

Genesis 14:18-20 And Melchizedek king of Salem brought forth bread and wine: and he was the priest of the most high God. And he blessed him, and said, Blessed be Abram of the most high God, possessor of heaven and earth: And blessed be the most high God, which hath delivered thine enemies into thy hand. And he gave him tithes of all.

Exodus 23:19-20 The first of the firstfruits of thy land thou shalt bring into the house of the LORD thy God. Thou shalt not seethe a kid in his mother's milk. Behold, I send an Angel before thee, to keep thee in the way, and to bring thee into the place which I have prepared.

Leviticus 27:30 And all the tithe of the land, whether of the seed of the land, or of the fruit of the tree, is the LORD's: it is holy unto the LORD.

Psalms 41:1 Blessed is he that considereth the poor: the LORD will deliver him in time of trouble.

Proverbs 3:5-10 Trust in the LORD with all thine heart; and lean not unto thine own understanding. In all thy ways acknowledge him, and he shall direct thy paths. Be not wise in thine own eyes: fear the LORD, and depart from evil. It shall be health to thy navel, and marrow to thy bones. Honor the LORD with thy substance, and with the firstfruits of all thine increase: So shall thy barns be filled with plenty, and thy presses shall burst out with new wine.

Proverbs 11:24-25 There is that scattereth, and yet increaseth; and there is that withholdeth more than is meet, but it tendeth to poverty. The liberal soul shall be made fat: and he that watereth shall be watered also himself.

Proverbs 28:27 He that giveth unto the poor shall not lack: but he that hideth his eyes shall have many a curse.

Malachi 3:6-12 For I am the LORD, I change not; therefore ye sons of Jacob are not consumed. Even from the days of your fathers ye are gone away from mine ordinances, and have not kept them. Return unto me, and I will return unto you, saith the LORD of hosts. But ye said, Wherein shall we return? Will a man rob God? Yet ye have robbed me. But ye say, Wherein have we robbed thee? In tithes and offerings. Ye are cursed with a curse: for ye have robbed me, even this whole nation. Bring ye all the tithes into the storehouse, that there may be meat in mine house, and prove me now herewith, saith the LORD of hosts, if I will not open you the windows of heaven, and pour you out a blessing, that there shall not be room enough to receive it. And I will rebuke the devourer for your sakes, and he shall not destroy the fruits of your ground; neither shall your vine cast her fruit before the time in the field, saith the LORD of hosts. And all nations shall call you blessed: for ye shall be a delightsome land, saith the LORD of hosts.

Matthew 6:1-4 Take heed that ye do not your righteousness before men, to be seen of them: else ye have no reward with your Father who is in heaven. When therefore thou doest alms, sound not a trumpet before thee, as the hypocrites do in the synagogues and in the streets, that they may have glory of men. Verily I say unto you, They have received their reward. But when thou doest alms, let not thy left hand know what thy right hand doeth: that thine alms may be in secret: and thy Father who seeth in secret shall recompense thee.

Matthew 6:19-21 Lay not up for yourselves treasures upon earth, where moth and rust doth corrupt, and where thieves break through and steal: But lay up for yourselves treasures in heaven, where neither moth nor rust doth corrupt, and where thieves do not break through nor steal: For where your treasure is, there will your heart be also.

Luke 6:38 Give, and it shall be given unto you; good measure, pressed down, and shaken together, and running over, shall men give into your bosom. For with the same measure that ye mete withal it shall be measured to you again.

Acts 20:35 I have showed you all things, how that so laboring ye ought to support the weak, and to remember the words of the Lord Jesus, how he said, It is more blessed to give than to receive.

Romans 15:26 For it hath pleased them of Macedonia and Achaia to make a certain contribution for the poor saints which are at Jerusalem.

1 Corinthians 13:3 And though I bestow all my goods to feed the poor, and though I give my body to be burned, and have not charity, it profiteth me nothing.

1 Corinthians 16:1-2 Now concerning the collection for the saints, as I have given order to the churches of Galatia, even so do ye. Upon the first day of the week let every one of you lay by him in store, as God hath prospered him, that there be no gatherings when I come.

2 Corinthians 9:6-7 But this I say, He which soweth sparingly shall reap also sparingly; and he which soweth bountifully shall reap also bountifully. Every man according as he purposeth in his heart, so let him give; not grudgingly, or of necessity: for God loveth a cheerful giver.

Galatians 6:9-10 And let us not be weary in well doing: for in due season we shall reap, if we faint not. As we have therefore opportunity, let us do good unto all men, especially unto them who are of the household of faith.

Ephesians 6:8 Knowing that whatsoever good thing any man doeth, the same shall he receive of the Lord, whether he be bond or free.

Philippians 4:10-19 But I rejoiced in the Lord greatly, that now at the last your care of me hath flourished again; wherein ye were also careful, but ye lacked opportunity. Not that I speak in respect of want: for I have learned, in whatsoever state I am, therewith to be content. I know both how to be abased, and I know how to abound: every where and in all things I am instructed both to be full and to be hungry, both to abound and to suffer need. I can do all things through Christ which strengtheneth me. Notwithstanding ye have well done, that ye did communicate with my affliction.

Now ye Philippians know also, that in the beginning of the gospel, when I departed from Macedonia, no church communicated with me as concerning giving and receiving, but ye only. For even in Thessalonica ye sent once and again unto my necessity. Not because I desire a gift: but I desire fruit that may abound to your account. But I have all, and abound: I am full, having received of Epaphroditus the things which were sent from you, an odor of a sweet smell, a sacrifice acceptable, wellpleasing to God. But my God shall supply all your need according to his riches in glory by Christ Jesus.

1 Timothy 6:17-19 Charge them that are rich in this world, that they be not highminded, nor trust in uncertain riches, but in the living God, who giveth us richly all things to enjoy; That they do good, that they be rich in good works, ready to distribute, willing to communicate; Laying up in store for themselves a good foundation against the time to come, that they may lay hold on eternal life.

Hebrews 7:2 To whom also Abraham gave a tenth part of all; first being by interpretation King of righteousness, and after that also King of Salem, which is, King of peace.

Hebrews 13:16 But to do good and to communicate forget not: for with such sacrifices God is well pleased.

1 John 3:17-18 But whoso hath this world's good, and seeth his brother have need, and shutteth up his bowels of compassion from him, how dwelleth the love of God in him? My little children, let us not love in word, neither in tongue; but in deed and in truth.

FAITH

Exodus 23:29-30 I will not drive them out from before thee in one year; lest the land become desolate, and the beast of the field multiply against thee. By little and little I will drive them out from before thee, until thou be increased, and inherit the land.

Numbers 23:19 God is not a man, that he should lie; neither the son of man, that he should repent: hath he said, and shall he not do it? or hath he spoken, and shall he not make it good?

2 Chronicles 20:20 And they rose early in the morning, and went forth into the wilderness of Tekoa: and as they went forth, Jehoshaphat stood and said, Hear me, O Judah, and ye inhabitants of Jerusalem; Believe in the LORD your God, so shall ye be established; believe his prophets, so shall ye prosper.

Psalms 37:3-5 Trust in the LORD, and do good; so shalt thou dwell in the land, and verily thou shalt be fed. Delight thyself also in the LORD; and he shall give thee the desires of thine heart. Commit thy way unto the LORD; trust also in him; and he shall bring it to pass.

Psalms 119:130 The entrance of thy words giveth light; it giveth understanding unto the simple.

Proverbs 16:3 Commit thy works unto the Lord, and thy thoughts shall be established.

Isaiah 55:11 So shall my word be that goeth forth out of my mouth: it shall not return unto me void, but it shall accomplish that which I please, and it shall prosper in the thing where-to I sent it.

Jeremiah 33:3 Call unto me, and I will answer thee, and show thee great and mighty things, which thou knowest not.

Matthew 17:20 And Jesus said unto them, Because of your unbelief: for verily I say unto you, If ye have faith as a grain of mustard seed, ye shall say unto this mountain, Remove hence to yonder place; and it shall remove; and nothing shall be impossible unto you.

Matthew 19:26 But Jesus beheld them, and said unto them, With men this is impossible; but with God all things are possible.

Matthew 21:22 And all things, whatsoever ye shall ask in prayer, believing, ye shall receive.

Mark 9:23 Jesus said unto him, If thou canst believe, all things are possible to him that believeth.

Mark 11:22-24 And Jesus answering saith unto them, Have faith in God. For verily I say unto you, That whosoever shall say unto this mountain, Be thou removed, and be thou cast into the sea; and shall not doubt in his heart, but shall believe that those things which he saith shall come to pass; he shall have whatsoever he saith. Therefore I say unto you, What things soever ye desire, when ye pray, believe that ye receive them, and ye shall have them.

John 14:13-15 And whatsoever ye shall ask in my name, that will I do, that the Father may be glorified in the Son. If ye shall ask any thing in my name,

I will do it. If ye love me, keep my commandments.

John 15:7 *If ye abide in me, and my words abide in you, ye shall ask what ye will, and it shall be done unto you.*

John 16:24 *Hitherto have ye asked nothing in my name: ask, and ye shall receive, that your joy may be full.*

Romans 10:17 *So then faith cometh by hearing, and hearing by the word of God.*

2 Corinthians 1:20 *For all the promises of God in him are yea, and in him Amen, unto the glory of God by us.*

2 Corinthians 5:7 *For we walk by faith, not by sight.*

Galatians 5:6 *For in Jesus Christ neither circumcision availeth any thing, nor uncircumcision; but faith which worketh by love.*

Ephesians 3:20 *Now unto him that is able to do exceeding abundantly above all that we ask or think, according to the power that worketh in us.*

Philemon 1:6 *That the communication of thy faith may become effectual by the acknowledging of every good thing which is in you in Christ Jesus.*

Hebrews 6:10-15 *For God is not unrighteous to forget your work and labour of love, which ye have shewed toward his name, in that ye have ministered to the saints, and do minister. And we desire that every one of you do shew the same diligence to the full assurance of hope unto the end: That ye be not slothful, but followers of them who through faith and patience inherit the promises. For when God made promise to Abraham, because he could swear by no greater, he sware by himself, Saying, Surely blessing I will bless thee, and multiplying I will multiply thee. And so, after he had patiently endured, he obtained the promise.*

Hebrews 10:35-36, 38 *Cast not away therefore your confidence, which hath great recompence of reward. For ye have need of patience, that, after ye have done the will of God, ye might receive the promise. . . . Now the just shall live by faith: but if any man draw back, my soul shall have no pleasure in him.*

Hebrews 11:6 *But without faith it is impossible to please him: for he that cometh to God must believe that he is, and that he is a rewarder of them that diligently seek him.*

James 2:26 *For as the body without the spirit is dead, so faith without works is dead also.*

1 John 3:22 *And whatsoever we ask, we receive of him, because we keep his commandments, and do those things that are pleasing in his sight.*

1 John 5:14-15 *And this is the confidence that we have in him, that, if we ask any thing according to his will, he heareth us: And if we know that he hear us, whatsoever we ask, we know that we have the petitions that we desired of him.*

God bless you as you go in peace to love and serve the Lord!

TO CONTACT THE AUTHORS

AL JANDL

Living Stones Church
1407 Victory Lane
Alvin, Texas
77511

Phone: 281-331-9517
Fax: 281-331-2653

Website:
www.livingstoneschurch.org

VAN CROUCH

Van Crouch Communications
P.O. Box 320
Wheaton, Illinois
60189

Phone: 630-682-8300
Fax: 630-682-8305

VanCrouch@aol.com

Website:
www.VanCrouch.com

BIBLIOGRAPHY

Bach, David. *The Automatic Millionaire: A Powerful One-Step Plan to Live and Finish Rich.* New York: Broadway Books, 2004.

Clason, George S. *The Richest Man in Babylon.* New York: Signet Books, 2002 (reissue).

Cole, Edwin Louis. *Communications, Sex, & Money: Overcoming the Three Common Challenges in Relationships.* Southlake, TX: Watercolor Books, 1987, 2002.

Kiyosaki, Robert. *Rich Dad, Poor Dad: What the Rich Teach Their Kids about Money—That the Poor and the Middle Class Do Not!* Scottsdale: TechPress, Inc., 1997, 1998.

Kiyosaki, Robert. *Cashflow Quadrant: Rich Dad's Guide to Financial Freedom.* New York: Warner Business Books, 2000.

Ramsey, Dave. *Financial Peace Revisited.* New York: Viking, 2003.

Ramsey, Dave. *The Total Money Makeover: A Proven Plan for Financial Fitness.* Nashville: Thomas Nelson, Inc., 2003.

Stanley, Thomas and Danko, William. *The Millionaire Next Door: The Surprising Secrets of America's Wealthy.* Atlanta: Longstreet Press, 1996.

Stanley, Thomas. *The Millionaire Mind.* Kansas City, MO: Andrews McMeel Publishing, 2000.

ABOUT THE WRITER: Rick and his wife, Melissa, operate Killian Creative, a freelance writing and consulting firm in Boulder, Colorado. They have two children. You can visit their website at www.KillianCreative.com.

THE CROSS STAFF was developed by Levi ben Gersohn around 1342. It was used by early explorers, and guided Columbus to the New World and the Pilgrims on the Mayflower to religious freedom. These early pioneers probably noticed an interesting aspect of this navigational tool—users looked through a cross to chart their course toward their destinations.

We at CrossStaff Publishers believe that it is through the cross of Jesus Christ that life's answers are found. It is our "moral compass." Just as ancient mariners had little room for excess baggage, we believe that readers want books that touch their hearts and deal with life's core issues. We trust this book will equip you to align your lives with the message of the cross of Jesus Christ. For without that cross, we would be adrift in the stormy sea of life. With it, we can navigate our way home to our Lord and Savior.

Additional copies of this book
are available at your local bookstore

CROSSSTAFF
PUBLISHERS, LLC

P.O. Box 288
Broken Arrow, Oklahoma 74013-0288